P9-CJH-166

Spies of the Revolution

by KATHERINE and JOHN BAKELESS

SCHOLASTIC INC.
New York Toronto London Auckland Sydney Tokyo

The materials in this book is based on TURN-COATS, TRAITORS AND HEROES, by John Bakeless. Copyright © 1959 by John Bakeless. Complete notes, documentary material, and bibliography will be found there. Spelling and punctuation of the Revolutionary period have been modernized in this book.

In this account the writers have concentrated upon material which is relatively unknown, and have passed over lightly the facts about espionage that can already be found in other books. The well-known story of Benedict Arnold and Major John André is only one example of this. The emphasis throughout the book is on the new; the old familiar spy stories of the Revolution are brought in only when they are necessary to an understanding of the whole story.

ISBN 0-590-01485-4

Copyright © 1962 by Katherine and John Bakeless. All rights reserved. This edition is published by Scholastic Inc., 730 Broadway, New York, N.Y. 10003, by arrangement with JB Lippincott Company.

22 21 20 19 18 17 16 15 14 13 12   4 5 6 7 8/8

Contents

I. SPIES IN MASSACHUSETTS, 1775

Tea or Coffee?   1
The Adventures of John Howe   27
The Paul Revere Gang   43
The Traitor Doctor   60

II. SPIES IN NEW YORK, 1776

Plots Within Plots   76
Nathan Hale—A Hero Wasted   92
Spiderweb of Spies   109

III. SPIES IN NEW YORK, NEW JERSEY, AND PENNSYLVANIA, 1776-1777

The Newest Secret Service   127
Codes, Masks, and Ciphers   151
The Wiles of Washington   164
Who's Got the Button?   172

IV. SUPER SPIES, 1778-1781

The Culpers' Secret Ink   187
The Tricky Double Agents   203

MAIN ACTION, AND SPIES ON EACH SIDE   219

This book begins on April 19, 1775, at the Battle of Lexington, where the American Revolutionary War began. It ends with the burning of New London by Benedict Arnold in 1781, the year the war really ended. In between it tells about the spy activity, both British and American, that helped shape events of the war in Massachusetts, New York, New Jersey, and Pennsylvania.

In the beginning, American spies were independent patriots, like Paul Revere. Later, Washington himself directed spy activity through his officers—and even took part by sending false information through enemy lines!

But whether the spies were ordinary citizens or highly placed officers, all helped to change the course of history. This is the story of those unsung heroes and silent villains of the American Revolution.

Tea or Coffee?

A COLUMN OF REDCOATS came marching up the road to Lexington. They were an advance guard, sent ahead to clear the way for more redcoats, following at some distance behind them.

On the green in Lexington the British soldiers found a company of American minutemen. There was some shooting. No one knows exactly who started it, but in a few minutes the green was dotted with American dead. Some wives saw their husbands being shot.

No redcoats were hurt at all. Lord Percy, commanding the advance guard, always insisted he gave no order to fire until after the minutemen had fired on the British soldiers. The Americans said the redcoats fired first. Probably those on each side thought they were telling the truth.

The fight at Lexington was really just a skirmish. It was all over in a few minutes, and those few minutes were so confused that no one knew exactly what did happen.

There is no doubt about one thing: the American Revolution began right there. Nor is there any doubt about something else: the British Empire really lost America forever in those few minutes on Lexington Common.

That is the story every American knows. And as far as it goes, it is a perfectly correct story of the Battle of Lexington. But there is more to it. We know something now that no one knew until a few years ago. The redcoats came to Lexington that April morning in 1775 because a British spy had sent a secret message to General Gage in Boston. The redcoats came without any artillery, only infantry—because a spy had told them the Americans wouldn't fight if there was no artillery in the British column. They just might, in fact, have saved the day for King George if they hadn't listened to their spy and had brought their cannon with them. In the end the redcoats had to send back to Boston for their big guns.

We know, too, that Paul Revere was able to make his famous ride and carry warning only because a daring group of American spies had been watching every British move for months.

But even that is only a part of the story, for

behind the fight at Lexington lay a long preparation for war by each side. Behind it also lies a
thrilling story of spying on both sides.

During the 1770's the colonists had been grow-
ing more and more determined to resist the
British government in defense of their fundamental liberties. They knew that resisting the
king was very likely to end in war. So did General Thomas Gage, British governor of Massachusetts and commander in chief of all the
British troops in North America.

Thus both sides knew that war might come,
and they began to get ready for it. The British
army was already organized and prepared to
fight. The Americans had to organize a new army
secretly—training men; buying powder, bullets,
and cannon; storing supplies of food. The best-
known American soldiers at this early stage were
the minutemen, so called because they were
ready to go at a minute's notice. But behind them
were other companies of soldiers, ready to follow and support the minutemen.

The military supplies for these soldiers had
to be prepared, then hidden and kept under
guard. General Gage, of course, wanted to seize
and destroy these American supplies, but first he
had to find them. He also had to find out the
secret plans of the American patriots. There was

only one way to do that. The general needed spies—and good ones.

Now England had had a first-class secret service for centuries. In Shakespeare's times Queen Elizabeth I was getting secret reports from all over Europe. Her spies, for instance, quickly discovered the plots to dethrone her and put Mary, Queen of Scots, on the throne of England.

Two hundred years later the English secret service was just as good. Daniel Defoe, who wrote *Robinson Crusoe*, was an English secret agent. Some people believe he was chief of the whole secret service.

But there had never been much British secret service in the American colonies, because there had never been much need of it. A few British spies had been at work during the French and Indian War. One of them once made a mistake and accused Colonel George Washington, commanding the Virginia militia, of being a French spy! (It was quite untrue, of course. The charges were dropped so quickly that Washington probably never even guessed he had been under suspicion.) Just after the French and Indian War, Gage suspected a Pennsylvania trader, Gershom Hicks, of being a spy—for the Indians. Gage wanted him hanged. But Hicks, who was probably innocent of spying for anybody at that time, managed to evade court-martial and survived. A few years later, during the Revolution, he really did spy—for the Americans, not the Indians.

Aside from these few instances, however, there was no active British espionage in the American colonies until signs of coming rebellion began to appear.

General Gage at first did not even have a code or a cipher, nor a single officer who knew how to make one. But as war began to draw nearer and nearer he had to know what the American patriots were plotting. As commander in chief, he wanted to know how many troops they had; how many cannon, muskets, rifles, bullets, bayonets, barrels of gunpowder; and how much food they had collected. The general also needed to know where all these military stores were hidden. If he could find and destroy most of the rebels' supplies, there would never be an American Revolution. The rebels would not fight, because they would have nothing to fight with.

Just exactly when General Gage set up the new British spy system in America, nobody knows. But it is perfectly certain that, for several months before Lexington, the British had some first-class spies snooping about among the American patriots. One of these was the prominent Boston physician, Dr. Benjamin Church, whom everybody considered one of the leading patriots.

What else could one think? Dr. Church was a close friend of such admired colonial leaders as the Adamses and Dr. Joseph Warren. His fellow citizens thought the doctor was so stanch a patriot that they elected him to the Massachusetts Provincial Congress, which was making the American war plans and buying and hiding the very supplies that General Gage wanted to know all about.

Another British spy was a young major in the New Hampshire militia. His name was Benjamin Thompson. (In afteryears he became Count Rumford, one of the most famous scientists in Europe.) Still another spy was a mysterious man living in Concord, Massachusetts, or very near it, who made all his reports in very bad French. No one to this day knows who he was, for he was never detected. Dr. Church and Count Rumford were not so lucky.

In addition to these spies, British officers and soldiers, disguised in civilian clothes, left Boston secretly from time to time to watch the minutemen at drill, or to slip into the patriots' storehouses and count their military supplies.

General Gage soon learned about patriot stores in other Massachusetts towns besides Concord. His spies reported there were supplies in Charlestown, Watertown, Worcester, Salem, Marblehead, Mystic, and Menotomy (present-day

Arlington). The general's information was very complete.

On February 21, 1775, his secret service reported that within five days twenty wagonloads of flour had gone from Marblehead to Salem, through Mystic, toward Worcester. The spies told him gun carriages were being made at Charlestown, Watertown, and Marblehead. They reported twelve brass cannon at Salem. They knew exactly where the guns were: "lodged near the North River, on the back of the Town." The spies said tools were being made at Menotomy, pickaxes at Mystic. It looked as if the largest of these Massachusetts supply dumps was at Worcester. Connecticut towns were also laying in food and ammunition, the largest supplies being at Hartford.

But it was not enough for the spies to find out where the patriots hid their supplies. Before General Gage could send his redcoats to seize these stores he needed professional observation by trained officers, both in Concord and Worcester, and along the roads his troops would have to travel.

General Gage sent his first pair of disguised soldiers toward Worcester on February 22, the day after receiving his intelligence reports, to be followed in April, after further alarming reports had come in, by a second pair. At about the same

time Major John Pitcairn, a very fine marine officer (who would command the advanced guard
at Lexington and die at Bunker Hill) put on
civilian clothes and went out to look things over
in Lexington and Concord.

As his first pair of spies in Worcester, General
Gage chose Captain William Brown and Ensign
Henry De Bernière. Since the British commander
knew only that there were supplies somewhere
in Worcester, his spies were to find out just
where in the town they were stored. The general
also required information about the roads; the
kind of country his troops would have to march
over; the bridges, woods, hills, defensible places
in the towns; possible spots for campsites; and
all about local supplies of food, forage, straw, and
extra horses.

With this in mind he sent out a call for officers
able to sketch maps of the country. De
Bernière was chosen because he could draw very
well. As these disguised officers were likely to
be seen at work, they were told to pose as surveyors. This was their "cover," to use a modern
word for an old trick.

The two officers, Brown and De Bernière, took
Captain Brown's soldier-servant, John, with them.
All three dressed as Yankee farm workers, in
rough brown clothes with handkerchiefs tied
around their necks. Leaving Boston, they passed

Cambridge—which they reported as "a pretty town, with a college built of brick" (Harvard)—and reached Watertown without being suspected. They stopped for dinner at Jonathan Brewer's tavern, just over the Watertown-Waltham boundary. They could hardly have made a worse mistake or selected a worse place, for the landlord was an ardent Whig. (Four months later, he was commanding American troops on Bunker Hill.)

While the two officers dined together, John went to the kitchen to have his meal with the other servants. This was their second mistake. Brown and De Bernière were waited on by a Negro girl who, as the secret agents noticed during dinner, began to eye them very closely. In their attempt to appear wholly at ease, though they were feeling nervous, they tried to talk with her.

One of them remarked that this was a very fine country.

"So it is," replied the girl, "and we have got brave fellows to defend it, and if you go up any higher you will find it so."

This answer unnerved the spies even more. Since General Gage had told them to pass for surveyors, they had casually placed some of their rough notes for a map upon the table for the girl to see. But she, not at all deceived, went straight back to the kitchen, where she told her suspicions. Captain Brown's servant, John, hearing her, warned his officers at once.

The spies hastily decided not to spend the night at the inn, as they had intended, but paid their bill and left as fast as possible. At a safe distance, they queried John about the girl. How much had she really guessed?

John said that "she knew Captain Brown very well, that she had seen him five years before at Boston, and she knew him to be an officer." She had guessed that their errand was to make military maps, because she had seen the river and road through Charlestown on their paper.

Although they were disturbed by this inauspicious beginning, the three men agreed it would be foolish to return to Boston now, with their mission unaccomplished. It was "necessary to push on to Worcester and run all risks rather than go back until we were forced."

Soon after leaving the tavern—was it really an accident?—they met a "country fellow" and another man who looked like a British deserter. These men wanted to "join company."

Going to Worcester?

Strangely enough, the dubious pair "were going our way," one officer wrote in his report.

This would never do. Even if their fellow travelers had been nothing more than what they said they were, the British agents dared not be seen making military maps. They shook off their unwanted acquaintances by stopping in Weston at the Golden Ball Tavern, kept by a notorious Tory, Captain Isaac Jones.

The two officers were relieved to see that innkeeper Jones was not inquisitive; they decided to stay the night, asked for a fire, and ordered coffee. This was the period of eighteenth-century coffeehouses in England. Maybe these two Englishmen really did like coffee as well as tea. But they certainly knew that, with the Boston Tea Party (December 6, 1773) only fourteen months in the past, no patriotic American was drinking tea. To ask for it openly would have been courting trouble in many a Yankee inn, but not in this one. Very quietly the landlord volunteered information:

"You may have what you please. Either tea or coffee."

This was a recognition signal, a quiet way of indicating that Captain Jones was loyal to the king. Tories had to be careful to whom they made such an offer. But innkeeper Jones appeared to realize that he was speaking to British officers. The captain and the ensign asked him to recommend safe inns on the road to Worcester. They dared not risk more trouble like that at Watertown. Jones told them to go to Buckminster's Tavern in Framingham, on the old

Boston-Worcester road, and to the house of another Jones, in Worcester. The gentlemen would
be safe, he said, under their Tory roofs.

The next day was rainy and freezing cold, the
kind of disagreeable, raw February day New
Englanders know too well. Most people were
staying snugly at home, and the road was so
nearly deserted that the spies could take their
time making sketches of the lay of the land, after
which they went on to Buckminster's. De
Bernière reported that "we felt very happy, and
Brown and I, and our man John, made a very
hearty supper; for we always treated him as our
companion, since our adventure with the black
woman." It had dawned on them at last that
genuine American farmers, traveling afoot, would
not be accompanied by a servant!

They reached Worcester with nothing to worry
about except a chance meeting with two men who
looked like deserters from the British army. If
the men really were deserters, they might recognize their former officers. At first the agents were
somewhat alarmed, but it turned out to be just
another of those anxious moments spies have to
face. Nothing happened, and the British officers,
after pausing to sketch a pass likely to be of
military importance, came safely to Worcester,
where they put up at the inn of the other Jones.

No one in Worcester paid any attention to

them, but it was evident that their host was
worried and not exactly glad to see them. He well
knew the risks he was running in receiving such
guests in that center of rebellion. "He seemed
a little sour, but it wore off by degrees," said
Ensign De Bernière afterward.

The next morning, when they asked what there
was for breakfast, the innkeeper gave the usual
Tory code: "Tea or coffee." This was an open
confession of the man's loyalty. But his guests
were careful to involve him as little as possible.
No questions were asked, no information given.
If the spies were caught, innkeeper Jones would
still not be involved.

As it was Sunday, the two disguised officers
dared not leave their lodging. Anyone walking
the streets during church services was likely to
be arrested. The two men kept out of sight till
sunset, the end of the Puritan Sabbath. After that,
secure in the early February dusk, they walked
freely about the town, seeing what they could
see. Then they went out on the hills sketching,
and returned safely to their lodging. It was presumably one or the other of these two spies who
made the plans for a camp and fortifications on
Chandler's Hill, outside Worcester. The plans
were found later after the British evacuated
Boston.

Presently the landlord announced that two

local gentlemen wished to speak with the travelers.

Who were they?

The landlord did not say, but he was sure his guests would "be safe in their company."

The intelligence agents took a cautious attitude. Their callers might be genuine Tories. On the other hand, they might be *provocateurs*—that is, a kind of double spy, an enemy agent who pretends to be a friend while trying to provoke some careless act that will give a spy away.

Assuming a casual attitude, the spies replied that of course they were safe. Why shouldn't they be safe? They were two private gentlemen. They were traveling merely to see the country. But they declined to see their callers, who, after an hour, went away.

The landlord, not offended and not at all deceived, chatted, talked politics, helped drink a bottle of wine, and explained, with a knowing air, that "none but a few friends to government" (meaning the British government, of course) knew of the officers' presence. The pair still feigned a calm they were far from feeling.

By the time they had secured their information and made their sketches, too many people were showing an interest in the captain and the ensign. They had stayed long enough. They started at daybreak for Framingham, where they wanted to make a few additional observations, since General Gage was likely to move his troops to Worcester that way. They took the precaution of carrying roast beef and brandy, so that there would be no need of stopping for meals at farmhouses where people might ask too many questions.

Beyond Shrewsbury, just east of Worcester, something happened that ought to have put them on their guard. They were overtaken by an unknown horseman. He examined the two pedestrians suspiciously and with unusual attention as he rode past. The man acted, Ensign De Bernière said later, "as if he wanted to know me again." He did, too.

The patriot Committee of Correspondence, far more alert than the officers realized, already knew that dubious strangers had been at Jones's tavern. The Committee had strong suspicions of their motives. In midwinter their pretense of being surveyors was hardly convincing. Road surveys, at best infrequent in Colonial Massachusetts, were not likely to be conducted at such a season.

Besides, the patriot leaders wondered why these two strangers were starting their "road survey" at Worcester. Why did they appear in town just as it was becoming a munitions center? The Committee wished it knew more about them. Captain Timothy Bigelow, commanding Worces-

ter's company of minutemen, had gone spy hunting to see what he could find out. The captain
was the horseman who had looked over the
British spies so carefully. He had then ridden
to Marlboro to prepare a warm reception for
them. But the officers saved themselves a great
deal of trouble (and perhaps their lives). They
decided to turn down the Framingham road,
thus accidentally evading Captain Bigelow.

Their next fright came at about six o'clock
when they got back to Buckminster's Tavern in
Framingham. They found a local militia company
drilling near it. When they saw the minutemen
march toward the tavern and continue their
drill right under the window of their room, the
uneasy spies again feared they had been discovered. But this too turned out to be mere
accident.

Fortune was certainly favoring the British spies
that day! By this lucky chance they were able
to listen to a speech by the company commander
to his men which gave the spies some idea of
the rebellious mood of the patriots. Then they
watched the militia drill, and gained firsthand
information for General Gage on the colonists'
military training. When the company was dis-
missed, the men came crowding into the barroom
to drink and talk till nine o'clock, unaware that
two British officers were watching them. So the

spies, with the minutemen close around them, had a chance to see exactly what their arms and equipment were. It would be very interesting information for General Gage, if his secret service officers ever got back alive to tell him.

Safely at the Golden Ball Tavern in Weston next day, Brown and De Bernière were warned by the innkeeper's family not to attempt any more trips into the country. But they were still not satisfied they had enough information about the northern road between Boston and Worcester, a road that General Gage might want to use. Disregarding the warnings, they started back along the upper road next morning. Since they now feared they might be arrested at any moment, they first gave their sketches and notes to their servant, John, and started him off to General Gage. If the patriots caught them now, their papers would still reach the general. There would be no incriminating documents on them to prove that they were spies. They would still be able to pose as private travelers.

Since it was snowing hard, people were keeping off the road. This made it possible for the two disguised officers to trudge along undisturbed until, about three miles east of Marlboro, another horseman caught up with them and paused to talk.

Where did they come from?

"Weston."

Did they live there?

"No."

Well, where did they live?

"At Boston."

Where were they going?

"To Marlboro, to see a friend."

Were they in the army? They denied it.

After several more questions the stranger rode on to Marlboro. Though the worried "surveyors" guessed that he would tell Marlboro patriots that suspicious-looking strangers were coming, there was only one thing they could do. They had to walk straight ahead, looking as innocent as possible. To turn around in the middle of the countryside and go the other way would only be a confession of guilt. They had to brazen it out. Dismally they footslogged ahead through driving snow, wondering what would happen when they reached Marlboro.

The town was ready for them when they tramped in. Everyone seemed to be waiting. Though it was snowing and blowing hard, people came out of their houses to watch.

"Where are you going, master?" a baker asked Captain Brown.

"To see Mr. Barnes," replied the captain truthfully.

Not a very helpful answer, since Barnes was a

notorious king's man; but there was no use lying —everyone could see where they went. The Marlboro patriots allowed them to enter Barnes's house.

The Englishmen apologized "for taking the liberty to make use of his house," adding that they were officers in disguise.

Barnes told them grimly that they did not need to tell him, since all Marlboro knew it. Patriots had been out hunting for them all night.

They asked if there was a safe tavern. No, certainly not. Where then? The safest place, Barnes told them, was in his house, right where they were. But they were far from feeling safe.

Barnes asked anxiously who had spoken to them as they entered the village.

"A baker."

"A very mischievous fellow," said Barnes, adding that "there was a British deserter at the baker's house."

Captain Brown asked the fellow's name.

"Swain," said Barnes. "He had been a drummer."

Brown looked glum. He knew Swain too well. He had deserted from Brown's own company a month before. He could not fail to recognize his former captain. As a deserter, Swain could best protect himself now by making trouble for Brown.

The two disguised officers asked Barnes, if the patriots got their hands on them, "what would they do with us?" The answer was not comforting. Barnes realized that whatever happened to the spies was likely to happen to him too, for harboring them.

Following this alarming conversation, Barnes was called out of the room. He returned more worried than ever. Dr. Samuel Curtis was selectman, town clerk, justice of the peace, and—this was the sinister part—a member of the patriot Committee of Correspondence. He had not been inside Barnes's house for the last two years. There could be only one reason why he appeared now. He came, said the ensign, "to see and betray us."

Barnes again left to talk with the intrusive physician. He regretted that "he had company and could not have the pleasure of attending him that night." Dr. Curtis was slow to take the hint. He did not go. He "stared about the house," no doubt hoping to see some revealing article that could be identified as part of a British uniform. Then he asked Barnes's little daughter who it was with her father.

The little girl said "she had asked her pappa, but he told her it was not her business." When the doctor at last departed, De Bernière gloomily assumed he went "to tell the rest of his crew."

All this had happened within twenty minutes. To remain there would be dangerous both to themselves and to their host, so Brown and De Bernière decided to leave. But as the two men had walked sixteen miles through the worst kind of New England winter weather, they needed food and an hour or two of rest.

Just as they were sitting down to a meal, Barnes rejoined them. He had gone to the kitchen to see what his servants had learned. He came back very uneasy. The patriots were going to raid his inn. There would be no safe place anywhere in Marlboro for the two officers that night.

The spies decided to leave instantly, though it was still snowing and blowing as much, De Bernière wrote later, as he had ever seen in his life. As they sneaked out of the house through the stables behind it, Barnes pointed out a back road that would take them around Marlboro at a distance of about a quarter of a mile. The Marlboro patriots had forgotten to block that back road.

As soon as they got to the hills overlooking the causeway at Sudbury, the Englishmen slipped into the woods to "eat a bit of bread," which they had brought along instead of dinner; but as their brandy was long since gone, they had to "eat a little snow to wash it down."

They had gone only about a hundred yards

farther when a man came out of a house and spoke to them.

"What do you think will become of you now?" he asked.

He may have meant it to be funny, in view of the foul weather, but to the anxious pair it sounded menacing.

By this time the two men were so nervous that, as De Bernière said, "our apprehensions made us interpret everything against us." This fear was heightened when they met a group of horsemen, who opened out to right and left of the road to let them through. This was, however, only courtesy, for these riders had no suspicions and did not try to stop the frightened spies.

Once more they reached the Golden Ball Tavern at Weston, after walking thirty-two miles. They had averaged four miles an hour "through a road that every step we sunk up to the ankles, and it blowing and drifting snow all the way." Innkeeper Jones gave them a bottle of mulled Madeira, after which they "slept as sound as men could do, that were very much fatigued."

The moment they had had breakfast the next morning, they pushed off to Boston. Jones had carefully pointed out a road that took them some distance below Watertown. Having been recognized there on the way out, they wisely "did not choose to go through that town."

As they came in sight of Boston, they met Generals Gage and Haldimand with their aides. The generals did not recognize their own spies.

A few days later, when Barnes, their Marlboro host, came to Boston, they learned how narrow their escape had been. They were lucky to have stayed in his house no longer than twenty minutes. The patriots had searched it "from top to bottom, looked under the beds and in the cellars." Convinced at last that their prey had given them the slip, the patriots had sent out horsemen in all directions. Ensign De Bernière was sure that he and Captain Brown had escaped only because the weather had been so very bad.

When General Gage saw how much useful intelligence the two officers had brought back from Worcester, he decided they might be equally successful in Concord. Less than a month before the fatal march to Lexington he ordered them "to set out for Concord, and examine the road and situation of the town." They were also to get what information they could about the artillery and provisions there.

In disguise once more, Captain Brown and Ensign De Bernière set off on a second espionage mission, this time taking the precaution of going armed. Brown's servant, John, was presumably with them, since the ensign reports, "We were three and all well armed."

Instead of taking the direct road northwest to Lexington, they went in the opposite direction— to Roxbury, then through Brookline, and then to the village of Weston (due south of Concord). This route avoided Jonathan Brewer's tavern with its dangerously observant young waitress. They reached Concord easily and made their observations safely before trouble began. As ordered, they observed rebel artillery. They found patriot troops on active duty in the village (though war had not begun). They watched American military routine: "They fired their morning gun, and mounted a guard of ten men at night." Clearly these men were there to guard American stores.

But with all their precautions, Captain Brown and Ensign De Bernière made one mistake that was very nearly fatal. They forgot that in Concord, where everyone knew what the patriots were doing, people were intensely suspicious. Daniel Bliss, a Harvard graduate, was the local Tory "contact man." But the spies had carelessly neglected to find out where he lived before they left Boston. As a result, they had to ask for him when they reached Concord.

They had just reached the Bliss house when the woman who had directed them to it appeared, weeping. She had been warned to leave Concord; otherwise she would be tarred and feathered "for directing Tories on their road." Bliss gave the spies dinner. Presently a threat reached him too. "They would not let him go out of the town alive that morning."

Dangerous as their position now appeared, Brown and De Bernière paused long enough to complete their task. They wanted to get an idea of the supplies the Provincial Congress had stored in Concord. The spies risked their lives to learn that flour for the rebel troops was being ground only two hundred yards away from the Bliss home. A harness shop nearby was making artillery harness and cartridge boxes. Besides flour, the stores included fish, salt, and rice. Bliss assured the two secret agents that the patriots would fight. As he was speaking, his own brother Thomas, a stanch patriot, passed by the house.

"There goes a man who will fight you in blood up to his knees," said Bliss.

The spies' lives had, of course, been in danger from the start. Now, since Bliss was in danger too, he decided to return to Boston with them. But in spite of the risk these officers never for a moment forgot their duty. On the way back through Lexington they took time to make a survey of the road, so that they could give a full and careful description of the very route the redcoats were to use.

On the night of April 18–19, 1775, Ensign De
Bernière was on this road again, guiding the
redcoat column to Lexington and Concord. Bliss
was safe in Boston with a job as commissary of
the British forces. When the war was over, he
would have to leave his New England home
forever.

The Adventures of
John Howe

Captain Brown and Ensign De Bernière had
hardly finished their espionage in Worcester
when other British spies began to report that the
patriots were collecting more military stores in
that town. Toward the end of March, 1775, General Gage knew he must have further information
regarding these stores. Since the supplies seemed
to be passing through Watertown and Weston
on their way to Worcester, he wanted to know
what was happening in those towns too.

Exactly two weeks before the Battle of Lexington and Concord, General Gage sent out a
second pair of secret agents. The two new spies
were Lieutenant Colonel Francis Smith, of the
Tenth Foot, and a younger man named John
Howe.

It is characteristic of the fate of secret agents
that John Howe, who succeeded brilliantly,
achieved no lasting fame and no promotion,
whereas Lieutenant Colonel Smith, after failing
as a spy and getting himself soundly defeated at
Concord, became a general. The colonel also
earned a permanent place in history, though not
a very glorious one. Howe did, however, make a
reputation in the secret service, and as the War
of 1812 approached, nearly forty years later, the
British sent him back to the United States on
another secret mission.

The two spies dressed as a pair of wandering
Yankee laborers, in leather breeches, gray coats,
"blue mixed" stockings, and handkerchiefs knot-
ted about their throats, and carried their luggage
tied up in large homemade handkerchiefs. Each
also had a foot traveler's stick. This could be
thrust through the knots of the kerchief so that
the wayfarer could carry his bundle over his
shoulder.

Starting before breakfast, they hiked through
Cambridge to Watertown. There Lieutenant
Colonel Smith's career as a secret agent came to
a swift and humiliating close. They stopped to
eat breakfast at the same Watertown tavern
where Brown and De Bernière had been spotted.
The British intelligence service had blundered

badly. No one had warned this second pair against the watchful Negro maid.

In an effort to keep up his pose as a laborer, Lieutenant Colonel Smith asked the girl where they could find work.

"Smith," said she, bluntly, "you will find enough employment for you and all General Gage's men in a few months."

The girl's reply was so completely startling that, Howe said, it "about wound up our breakfast."

The girl must have enjoyed the impression she created, for, as Howe later remarked, "Smith appeared thunderstruck."

When their host came around to inquire how their breakfast suited them, one spy replied, "Very well, but you have got a saucy wench there."

The landlord, trying to smooth matters over, agreed that the girl was indeed a saucy creature. He explained, "She has been living in Boston, and has got acquainted with a great many British officers and soldiers." Was it accident or sly malice that made him add, eyeing their costume, "and she might take you to be some of them"? Hastily paying their bill, Smith and Howe departed, as if to follow their landlord's suggestion that they might "find work up the road."

Once on the road, the crestfallen pair hurried

as fast as they could, but not in quest of work.
Lieutenant Colonel Smith and John Howe wanted
to put as much distance as possible between
themselves and that tavern. As soon as they were
out of sight, they climbed over a stone wall and
settled down behind it to discuss matters. Since
both agreed it was useless for Lieutenant Colonel
Smith to continue, he decided to hurry back to
the British army in Boston. He gave Howe their
"journal book," a pencil, ten guineas, and letters
to various Tories. (A secret agent should carry
his information in his head, never on paper. If
discovered, that journal book would convict
Howe of espionage. The letters would convict all
the persons to whom they were addressed.) In
parting, Lieutenant Colonel Smith remarked that
if he ever came back over the road with his regiment, he would "kill that wench." But, when he
did march out of Boston again, on his way to
Lexington, his troops took another road. After
promising Howe a commission if he came back
alive, the colonel started back toward Boston.

Howe went on toward Waltham alone, making
a pretense of asking for work. He was shrewd
enough to drop the casual remark that he was
a gunsmith by trade. That, he knew, was the
surest way to learn about rebel arms. At Waltham, hearing this, a farmer directed him to
Springfield, where, he said, they needed hands

to work at that business, adding that Howe had better hurry because the patriots expected they would be needing guns very soon. "They mean to be ready for them," the farmer added.

Howe was delighted to secure this information so easily. It was important to know that the rebels had set up an arms factory in Springfield, and that they were working fast, as if expecting war very soon. What the farmer told him was proof that the patriots *would* fight. It also sounded as if the Americans expected the redcoats to move far west into Massachusetts, against Springfield. All that would interest General Gage. Two weeks later, when Gage did march troops out against the Americans, he did not move west toward Springfield (where he might be expected). He moved northwest against Concord.

Howe was clever enough to hide his satisfaction from the farmer. He was careful to keep up his disguise, too. When, a moment later, the talkative farmer asked if he would like a drink, Howe asked for something no Englishman would ever drink. He said he'd like a glass of "New England and molasses." This meant a mixture of rum and molasses which, as he noted down, he well knew to be a "Yankee drink."

Going on, he presently came to a causeway— that is, a road raised above the level of marshy ground—and stopped to study it. General Gage would want to know if it could carry artillery. A man who was setting traps there asked what he was looking for. The question seemed to be prompted merely by friendliness, not by suspicion; but whichever it was, Howe, as usual had an answer ready. He was trying to find sweet flag, a swamp iris whose root was supposed to cure a stomachache. The trapper offered to show him where the plant grew, and remarked, as they passed a large buttonwood tree, that "the people were going to cut it down to stop the regulars from crossing with their cannon."

This was just the kind of information that Howe had been sent to learn: (a) there would be resistance near Waltham; (b) passage of artillery and transport could be easily blocked; (c) British engineers would need plenty of axes to clear the way.

Since it is a mistake to ask too many questions, Howe ventured only one more: how would the people know when the regulars were coming?

"They had men all the time in Cambridge and Charlestown looking out," answered the trapper. Before parting, he directed the spy to two taverns, one "by Weston meeting house," the other "half a mile above." The first "was kept by Mr. Joel Smith, a good tavern and a good liberty man; the other was kept by Captain Isaac Jones, a wicked Tory, where a great many British officers go from Boston."

Howe already knew all about that loyal subject of King George, Captain Isaac Jones. He was the innkeeper who had already helped Brown and De Bernière. In fact Howe had in his pocket a letter to Jones, from General Gage himself.

Thinking it less suspicious to head straight for the tavern of the "good liberty man," Howe stepped up to the door just as two teamsters were harnessing their horses. These men had driven their loads out from Boston that morning, had paused for a midday meal in the tavern, and were now ready to go on. Along the way they had heard stories about suspicious travelers at Watertown, so when they saw John Howe they had their doubts. They accused him of being British, not of being a spy, though in early 1775 and in the vicinity of Boston the two were usually the same. They said he "looked like them rascals they seen in Boston."

To disarm suspicion, Howe hastily ordered another "Yankee drink." Then he gabbled on about gunsmithing in Springfield. Finally Howe added that he wanted work—any kind—because he needed money.

This sounded all right to Yankee ears. Wayfarers looking for jobs were common enough. Moreover, to Howe's great relief, the patriots told

him he would probably find work at the tavern of
Captain Isaac Jones, thus providing him with a
fine excuse for visiting the very Tory he wanted
to see.

Little did the spy realize that the local patriots
could also play a few tricks. They knew that if
this stranger really was a British secret agent,
he would surely want to get in touch with Captain Jones. They sent him there so that they
would know where to find him.

Handing Jones his letter from General Gage,
Howe told the Tory innkeeper about his mission
and what had happened at the other tavern.
Jones knew better than to take chances, and so
saved himself from a coat of tar and feathers.
He ordered his hired man to conduct this dangerous visitor to a remote house belonging to
Wheaton, another Tory, whom Jones knew he
could trust. When the hired man told Wheaton
frankly that Howe was a British agent, the hos-
pitable Loyalist provided a private room, candles,
paper, and brandy.

Howe settled down to write some notes on the
information he had now collected. This was, of
course, the wrong thing to do. He should have
carried it back to General Gage in his head. If he
were caught and searched, these notes would be
found on him and might easily hang him.

Meantime news spread that the keen-eyed

waitress at Watertown had recognized a British officer in disguise. No one knew that Lieutenant Colonel Smith had gone back to Boston, so the patriots were looking for two spies.

In a short time thirty angry citizens were clamoring at Jones's tavern, charging him with hiding British spies.

Blandly Captain Jones invited the men to search his house. No one there! Stung by their failure to uncover a spy or two, the patriots began questioning Jones's servant woman.

Were there strangers or Englishmen in the house?

She hardly thought so.

Had there been any?

One or two gentlemen had dined upstairs.

Where had they gone?

To Jericho Swamp, two miles away.

Suspicion began to die down. Captain Jones helped it die with a free bottle of spirits.

Undisturbed by this excitement, safe in the Wheaton house, Howe spent a few quiet hours noting in his journal some additional information —thoughtfully supplied by Jones—about the local militia. He had dinner, was introduced to the Wheaton daughters as "a British officer in disguise," played cards with them, and also drank "a dish of tea."

Once more the patriots tried a trick. Though

they had ostentatiously left the Tory tavern after searching it, they secretly kept it under observation, hoping to trap Howe should he venture to return. Captain Jones, aware of all this, sent his hired man to guide Howe from the Wheaton house along a back road to the main Worcester road. The two forded Sudbury River, some miles from Framingham, and went on to Marlboro, keeping on back roads or cross-country paths all the way.

Waking Barnes, the Marlboro Tory, they showed him two letters to convince him of their good faith. One was the letter General Gage had given Howe, the other was a special letter Jones had given his hired man. Barnes took them in and gave them refreshment. He told them that the news of the Watertown spy scare had already reached Marlboro, but local people didn't believe it. After hearing this, the hired man departed, since it was dangerous for any member of a Tory household to be conspicuously absent from home for any length of time. The sooner he was back where he belonged, the better it would be. Howe got to bed about four in the morning.

Barnes waked him at nine with bad news. During their night journey Howe and the hired man had been seen by a woman "up with a sick child." In the prevailing atmosphere of general suspicion, she leaped to the correct conclusion that these were spies and watched long enough to see that they went toward Worcester. Barnes had gone to the local tavern while his secret guest was sleeping, and there had picked up word of this approaching danger.

During the day Howe could do nothing but stay indoors and keep away from windows. Barnes went back to the tavern for more gossip. He returned about four in the afternoon with the news that the spy scare had now "turned out to be servants' stories," not generally believed. None the less, it was high time for Howe to leave. At eight o'clock that evening he started for Worcester, only about fifteen miles away, riding Barnes's horse and examining roads and bridges as well as he could in the darkness.

In Worcester a Tory who was another link in General Gage's secret-service chain sheltered Howe, after examining the letters he carried from the general and Barnes. This Tory (given no name in Howe's report) hid the spy in a private room all day, supplied information about local militia strength and munitions stores, and after dark took him to see the unguarded American magazine. His host also showed the spy two old wells where the British raiders could dump flour and gunpowder when the time came.

Howe collected his notes and started back from Worcester to the Barnes inn at Marlboro. As he rode along through the darkness, he grew fearful and depressed. He wrote later, "I was now fifty miles from Boston, and in danger of being captured every moment. The night was long and dismal. I often wished this night that I had never undertaken the business of a spy." Many another spy since then has felt the same way.

But luck rode with him. Except for an unseasonably heavy April snowfall, "nothing particular took place during the night," he reported.

Near dawn, Howe drew rein at Barnes's door in Marlboro for the second time. After eating a warm breakfast and turning his papers over to his host for safekeeping, Howe went to bed. Again the cautious Barnes went to the local tavern to see what he could learn, returning at one o'clock to tell Howe that, though everything was quiet, he had best not tarry for the night.

After dinner the spy took back his papers and added to his notes more information which Barnes had collected while Howe himself had been at Worcester. He now had a full report for his general. Howe prepared to be on his way to Boston and safety.

From an attic window Barnes pointed out a safe route to Concord, "across the lots and the road." About eight o'clock, when Howe had planned to start, came a knocking on the front door. As Barnes rose to answer, he told his guest that if he heard anything suspicious as the door opened, he was to slip out the window, climb down a shed roof, head for the neighboring swamp, and thence make his way to Concord.

A moment after his host had gone downstairs, the spy heard a strange voice below.

"We have come to search your house for spies," it said.

Then he heard Barnes say, "I am willing."

Was he going to be caught at last, after all his information was ready for General Gage? Howe pushed up the window, stepped out into six inches of snow, crawled along the roof, slipped, then fell to the ground, flat on his back.

Fortunately for Howe, the amateur spy catchers thundering on the front door made so much noise themselves that they heard nothing; nor had they taken the elementary precaution of surrounding the house first! Picking himself up, Howe raced for the swamp. There, looking back at Barnes's house, he could see "lights dodging at every window" and could hear horses in the road. The horses must have obscured his footprints in the snow, since there was no pursuit.

Howe knocked at a strange house, found it occupied by a Negro man and his wife, and was invited to stay the night. But he said that his business was urgent, and offered them money if they would put him on the road to Concord.

The man not unnaturally wondered what business was urgent enough to force anyone to travel afoot on such a night. The spy told the same story that had served a few days before. He was "going to make guns to kill the regulars" (British).

The couple hesitated. They had been hearing local rumors. The spy story had turned into a soldier story. The woman said she had heard there had been a number of regulars around Squire Barnes's house a day or two earlier. Howe looked amazed, and asked if Squire Barnes was really a Tory. Indeed he was! Then, said Howe, venomously, "he hoped they would catch him and hang him."

As this sounded like the proper sentiment, the man set out to guide the spy. He borrowed a canoe from another Negro at the Concord River and paddled Howe safely across, after which he offered to go a little farther, for more money. About midnight they came to a tavern, where they spent the night. Next morning Howe succeeded in convincing some Concord patriots that he was the gunsmith they needed. When they brought him several gunlocks and found a shop for him to work in, he made the repairs quickly, "considering the tools I had to work with," he noted in his report. It was very convincing.

After dinner his confiding American friends showed the British secret agent the Concord magazine of military stores. So for a second time Howe was able to walk right up and examine a patriot munitions dump!

Explaining that he must go "down East" to fetch his own gunsmith's tools, Howe left the gullible Americans at Lincoln, a few miles away, and took refuge with a Tory named Gove. This man had been in the vicinity of Barnes's house during the patriots' raid. For the first time Howe heard about the tar and feathers that the patriots had ready to use if they caught him. Gove sheltered him in an outbuilding, and the next day he helped him get additional information, and that night drove him to Charlestown. By two o'clock in the morning Howe was across the Charles River and safely back in his own quarters in Boston, his mission accomplished.

Putting on his British uniform again and starting down the street next morning, the triumphant spy met Lieutenant Colonel Smith, who greeted him with, "How do you do, John? We heard you broke your neck jumping out of Barnes's chamber window."

The speed with which this news got back to Boston shows there was another British intelligence net in Worcester.

Howe went with Smith to report to General Gage, turned in his papers at last, and was promised a bonus of fifty guineas.

A week later General Gage's redcoats were on the march to Lexington and Concord. But thanks to Paul Revere's ring of spies the patriot minutemen were waiting for them, and the artillery and munitions in Concord which the British spies Brown, De Bernière, and Howe had reported upon had already been moved to new hiding places. The British got such a beating on this march that they had to give up their raid on Worcester. All the work the spies had done, all the risks they had run, were wasted.

The Paul Revere Gang

However active British espionage may have been, the Americans had plenty of spies too. In fact they had so many that the patriots in Boston and Concord usually knew as much about the British as Gage and his staff knew about the patriots.

There had been an organized and active American secret-service ring in Boston ever since the autumn of 1774. Perhaps it had been working against the British even earlier. This American espionage network began as one of those volunteer groups of amateur secret agents that spring up naturally in invaded countries. It was very like the French resistance group that proved so useful to the Allies in World War II.

This American intelligence net, the first one
ever known, was set up by Paul Revere and about
thirty others. These men were described as
"mechanics." That is, they were skilled workmen
of one kind or another, like Paul Revere himself.
Their purpose, Revere reported, was "watching
the movements of the British soldiers, and gain-
ing every intelligence of the movements of the
Tories." As the fateful spring of 1775 drew on,
these Boston volunteers "frequently took turns,
two and two, to watch the soldiers, by patrolling
the streets all night."

The patriotic plotters had the advantage such
local spy systems always have. They needed no
cover to explain their presence in Boston. They
were all well-known local men. Revere himself
was a distinguished craftsman, whose exquisite
silverware was already displayed in fine New
England homes. They had friends whose houses
could give shelter and concealment in emer-
gencies. They knew the little byways of the city
better than any redcoat could possibly know
them.

Paul Revere himself carried so many messages
for the Americans that General Gage's staff soon
guessed what he was doing. But Revere did it
so cleverly that he was never arrested until the
night he made his famous ride. Even then the
British officers who caught him soon let him go.

It is surprising that more members of the patriotic Boston spy ring were not discovered, but the British seem never to have disturbed them. One reason was that their quiet nightly reconnaissance was divided among some thirty spies, working in pairs. The same men were not likely to be on the prowl oftener than once a fortnight. British intelligence officers knew well enough something was going on. They even knew some of the secret information the spies gathered. But, until the war began, they never caught a single American secret agent.

However, Paul Revere's group had the faults, as well as the advantages and enthusiasm, of all amateur secret agents. Their worst mistake was failing to conceal the identity of their members. The one fundamental rule in secret service is that, except for messengers and immediate associates, the various secret agents must never meet. They must never even know each other.

The whole network of eager Boston spies, however, instead of guarding their anonymity, held regular meetings at the Green Dragon Tavern. Though well aware of the need for secrecy, they had no idea how to achieve it. Their only precaution was to take an oath at each meeting, swearing to reveal their work to no one except a small group of patriot leaders. Unfortunately one of those supposed patriot leaders was really a British spy!

Because of this, it is hard to understand how any of Revere's secret group escaped with their lives. But fortunately for the American cause, neither General Gage nor the traitorous "patriot" who was secretly spying for him knew much about military intelligence themselves.

Though he certainly betrayed to General Gage the reports the patriot spies tried so hard to keep secret, Gage's spy seems never to have revealed the names of any of Revere's secret agents. He thus let slip a perfect chance to wipe out the whole Paul Revere spy net.

The British knew something of Paul Revere's activity as a messenger for the patriots, but they had no idea how much espionage he and his associates were really carrying on. Nor did they know who was responsible for the constant sabotage—undoubtedly the work of the Revere gang —in and around Boston. In mid-September, 1774, American secret agents "spiked up" all the British guns in Boston's North Battery.

Artillery in those days was fired by applying a match to the powder in a "touch hole" at the rear of the gun. To make it impossible to fire the cannon, all you had to do was to drive an iron spike (or an old bayonet) into the touch hole. Besides spiking those guns in this way, the raiding American saboteurs dropped others into a mill pond.

At about the same time two brass field guns disappeared from a Tory artillery company. The battery commander, Major Adino Paddock, put his two remaining guns under guard. They, too, disappeared from under the very noses of the guard. Before long all four of Major Paddock's guns turned up in the American artillery at Concord!

Early in December, 1774, the Revere gang learned that General Gage meant to send two regiments to Portsmouth, New Hampshire. They were to guard the powder stored in a British fort there. With such a force protecting the powder, the Americans would never be able to steal it. Paul Revere rushed off with a prompt warning. That night a few New Hampshire patriots went down the river in a little boat, waded ashore, attacked the small garrison before the additional redcoats had arrived, and carried off about a hundred barrels of powder. It is said some of this very powder was used against the British at Bunker Hill, a few months later.

The ease with which Gage's spies had penetrated American secrets should have warned him that his own secrets might also leak. But as we have said, he and his officers seem to have had no idea how completely they were being spied upon.

They were shockingly careless, for example, in not concealing their preparations for the march to Lexington and Concord. It was easy enough for Revere's men to know what was coming, because both Admiral Graves and General Gage all but gave the rebels warning of what they meant to do. On April 15 the admiral ordered all small boats lowered from the transports in the Charles River and left floating under their sterns. For three days they were in full view from both banks.

In those days, before the "made" land of the Back Bay section had been filled in, the city of Boston stood on the round end of a peninsula shaped like a frying pan. It was connected with the mainland by the long, narrow strip then known as Boston Neck. The watching Americans knew that troops would use the boats to cross the Charles River only if they were going to march northwest to Concord. If they intended to march west to Worcester, they would take the easier route—by land, down Boston Neck.

So by April 16, the day after Admiral Graves had slung out his boats, Revere's intelligence net knew the British would raid Concord. Revere himself rode to Lexington to warn John Hancock and Samuel Adams, who had been attending the Massachusetts Provincial Congress there and were about to start to Philadelphia to attend the

Second Continental Congress. Both were guests
in the Lexington parsonage of the Reverend Jonas
Clark.

Concord was immediately warned. Ox teams
began to haul stores away. Patriot artillery was
carted off to new hiding places. Bullets were
put in sacks and hidden in swamps. The time
was too short to move everything. But the detailed reports which Gage's secret agents—Brown,
De Bernière, and John Howe—had so recently
collected were almost entirely out of date by
the time the British troops arrived only three
days later.

Paul Revere rode quietly back to Boston, stopping at the Charlestown home of Colonel William
Conant to make a plan. From Charlestown the
steeple of Christ Church (now known as the
Old North Church) was plainly visible. Revere
told Colonel Conant that his group would show
one lantern in the steeple if the British went
"by land"—that meant over Boston Neck. They
would show two lanterns if they "went out by
water"—that is, across the Charles River.

Of course there was never any possibility that
the British troops would go, as Paul Revere says
in the Longfellow poem, "by sea." Neither Lexington nor Concord is anywhere near salt water.
Longfellow used poetic license, because he
needed to finish a stanza with a rhyme for the

line "I on the opposite shore will be." But even
that was wrong. Revere did not really wait on the
opposite shore, or on any shore. He was still in
the city of Boston, and very busy at the Old
North Church itself, when the famous lanterns
gleamed from its steeple. In fact Revere helped
hang the lanterns. At least he went as far as the
church door with the man who did hang them.

The lights were actually meant, not for Paul
Revere, but for Colonel Conant in Charlestown.
The signals had to be agreed on in advance because, as Revere himself explained after the war,
the British might put such a tight guard on the
city that American messengers would not be able
to ride down Boston Neck or row across the
Charles River. General Gage could put a line of
sentries across the Neck. Admiral Graves could
keep enough guard boats in the river to stop
any American boats that tried to cross. But even
if no patriot messenger could get out of Boston
after the British troops started to move, the lanterns could still flash their warning.

With these arrangements all made, Paul Revere
went home. For some months he had had a little
boat safely hidden away, to be used the moment
the redcoats started to move. On the famous
night of April 18, 1775, the British took all the
steps Paul Revere had expected. General Gage
did try to cut off Boston's land communications

by putting roadblocks on Boston Neck. Admiral Graves did try to cut off the city's water communications by having H.M.S. *Somerset* anchored in the mouth of the Charles River. But Paul Revere and his secret agents were ready for them. In spite of all Gage and Graves could do, William Dawes managed to pass the guard on Boston Neck. Revere himself slipped across the Charles River, past H.M.S. *Somerset*, in his boat. Even if both patriots had failed, the signal lanterns would still have blazed their message to Colonel Conant on the other bank.

General Gage expected no trouble. He thought his men could reach Concord, destroy American munitions, and be safely back in Boston before the alarm could be spread. But this time Gage's spies failed. His soldiers never knew—till it was too late—that the minutemen had been alerted and were ready for them.

The patriots, on the other hand, were very well informed. Almost everyone in Boston knew, almost as soon as the orders were issued, that the redcoats were going to march. People knew (or guessed correctly) exactly where they were going to march.

This was partly because British officers talked carelessly. Many of them were living in American private houses, where everything they did or said was observed and reported. In fact Major John

Pitcairn, the British marine officer who was second in command on the march to Lexington, was living almost next door to Paul Revere. To make matters worse, some of the British soldiers' wives worked as housemaids in American homes. There was bound to be loose talk.

The moment the soldiers began to get ready, the secret was out. It is nearly impossible to conceal the fact that troops are going to move. They have to assemble. They have to fall in. They have to march off. And in a city like Boston people could easily see all they did.

As day melted into evening and then into night on April 18, 1775, everybody in Boston was on edge. Something was going to happen, and nearly everybody knew what it was. It was a busy time for spies. After a conference with General Gage in the Province House, Lord Percy walked down to Boston Common to look over the troops. He did not then guess that within a few hours he would be leading the reinforcements rushed out from Boston to rescue these very redcoats from the minutemen. The Boston people did not recognize him, for his scarlet uniform was covered with a cloak, and looked by night very much like civilian clothing.

A voice came from the darkness: "The British troops have marched, but will miss their aim."

"What aim?" asked the startled nobleman.

"Why, the cannon at Concord," said the voice.

Percy hurried back to tell his general that their important military secret had already leaked out. But it was too late to halt the raid on Concord. They could only hope the news had not reached the minutemen.

It hadn't—yet.

But as soon as Dr. Joseph Warren, president of the Massachusetts Provincial Congress, was sure the redcoats were going to march, he started William Dawes off on horseback. Though Boston Neck was guarded, the sentry at the roadblock happened to be a friend. He let Dawes through. About ten o'clock Dr. Warren, still worried, sent for Paul Revere. He knew Hancock and Adams, though warned two days earlier, were still at Parson Clark's in Lexington. As Dawes might not get through, Revere must take a second warning.

First, however, those lanterns must be hung in the Old North Church. Colonel Conant was waiting to see the signal flash out. Revere hunted up his friend Robert Newman. He was sexton of the church, and was expecting Revere. Newman lived with his mother, in whose house British officers were quartered. He had gone to bed early that night, slipped out through a window, crossed a roof, and dropped into the dark street, where he waited in the shadows till Paul Revere came. Together they went to get John Pulling, a vestry-

man of the church, and also perhaps Revere's
neighbor, Thomas Barnard. It was probably Newman who actually went up the narrow stairway,
past the church's eight bells, and on to the top
of the belfry.

Two lanterns had been stored in the church.

The lanterns shone out. How long, no one
knows. Probably not very long, because Pulling
was "afraid that some old women would see the
light and scream fire," and the lookout on the
British ship *Somerset*, in the river just below,
might raise an alarm. Indeed there must have
been some kind of disturbance in front of the
church very soon, because Newman left the
church through a back window instead of the
front door. Slipping quietly home, he returned
by the roof-and-window route to his bedroom.
He lay awake, too excited to sleep, listening to
some British officers laughing over their card
game in the room downstairs.

As soon as the British learned of the signals,
Newman was arrested. Under questioning, he was
oh, so innocent!

What had *he* done?

Nothing. Pulling had asked him for the keys
to the church.

But it was late at night.

Well, Pulling was a vestryman. Newman was
only a sexton; he had to do what the vestryman

asked. He had turned over the keys and gone to bed.

He really had gone to bed, too. The officers living in the house could testify to that, if anybody asked them. True, he hadn't stayed in bed. But the officers didn't know that. In the end the British had to let him go. Newman could say what he pleased without any danger to Pulling, for the vestryman had left Boston for a safer place where the British could not get their hands on him.

Revere himself went safely home, but he had difficulty leaving again for his famous ride. By this time British troops were falling in near his house. No one was allowed through their ranks. Somehow Paul Revere finally slipped away, but he left without his spurs. They might have been hard to explain, if he had been stopped. His dog followed him out of the house.

Down at the river's edge the boat builder, Joshua Bentley, and Thomas Richardson were waiting to row Revere across the Charles. All these men helping Revere that night were obviously members of his patriotic group of "mechanics" and spies.

Revere appeared according to plan. Only then did the three remember that they would need a cloth to muffle the oars. One of them knew a girl who lived near by, at the corner of North and

North Centre streets. He walked quietly under
her window and gave a special whistle. The window moved up silently. There were whispers.
Then a flannel petticoat came floating down.

This tale, which Paul Revere told his children
later on, was easy to believe. But then he
stretched it a little—for their delight, no doubt—
by saying he had sent his dog home with a note
to his wife, and the dog came back carrying his
spurs.

Silently the oars, muffled with that flannel petticoat, pushed the little boat past the looming bulk
of the big ship *Somerset*, with her sixty-four guns.
The lookout and the officer of the deck failed to
see anything. One can imagine the three men
in the boat holding their breath as they floated
past in the darkness.

At Colonel Conant's home a group of patriots
were waiting. They had already seen the signal
lights in the Old North Church's steeple. There
was a hasty consultation. Paul Revere would
need a good horse. A wealthy citizen named
John Larkin gave him the best mount in his
stable.

Everyone knows the rest of that thrilling story,
"the midnight ride of Paul Revere"—how he was
almost caught near Cambridge but escaped
"cross-country"; how he "alarmed almost every
house"; how Hancock wanted to stay and fight

in Lexington; how William Dawes, the patriots'
second messenger, rode up to the Reverend
Mr. Clark's house half an hour after Revere got
there; how both Revere and Dawes then rode on
toward Concord together with young Dr. Samuel
Prescott, who had been calling on a girl in Lexington; how Paul Revere was caught and Dawes
driven off, while Prescott's horse jumped a fence
and got him through to Concord with a warning;
how Dawes lost his watch in the excitement, but
found it again a few days later.

The British major who captured Revere soon
decided it was better to let him go. There was no
charge on which he could be held. But the British
kept his horse—Larkin's horse, rather—and Revere
had to get back to Lexington on foot. He arrived
at the parsonage for the second time, to find Hancock still full of fight. It was dawn before that
statesman could be persuaded to get on his way
to Woburn and thence to Philadelphia, where
he was really needed. Paul Revere helped hide
Hancock's papers.

Somewhere along the road John Howe, Gage's
favorite secret agent, had again donned "Yankee
dress" and was out rousing Tories, exactly as Revere had been rousing patriots. But John Howe
was a little late.

As they marched along through the night, the
British soldiers could hear alarm guns, church

bells, and drums here and there, all around them. Their general's plan to surprise Lexington and Concord had failed. The Paul Revere gang had seen to that. Now there would be a fight. More troops would be needed. A courier was sent back to Boston, asking for reinforcements. Lord Percy hurried out from Boston, bringing up the re- serves—eight hundred more redcoats, this time with artillery.

Unknown to the British, as they approached Lexington Common, a man looked down at them from a window in Buckman's Tavern. It was Paul Revere.

So began the day on which would ring out the "shot heard round the world." All Europe was watching those dauntless American patriots who, eight years later, after a long and terrible war, would produce a new and democratic nation. One European government was watching closer than the rest of Europe. One king had his men right there.

Paul Revere was not the only silent watcher. Somewhere in Lexington two spies of Louis XVI, King of France, were quietly watching too. These French intelligence agents were Achard de Bon- vouloir and the Chevalier d'Amboise. They had come up from the West Indies to see what was really happening in the British colonies, and they stayed for a while to observe the first stages of the siege of Boston, after Lexington and Concord. Then they went on to London to report to the French ambassador there—not, for some reason, to Paris, where they could have reported to their own government.

Obviously pleased with the intelligence they brought, the ambassador sent de Bonvouloir back across the Atlantic to continue to find out what the Americans were doing.

The French government was being correctly neutral, though still smarting from its defeat, at the hands of the British, in the French and Indian War a dozen years before. Three years later, in 1778, France was to come to the aid of the American colonies. This led to Yorktown and victory. Perhaps that secret mission of de Bonvouloir was one of the most important of the whole war, though at the time no one knew anything about it.

The Traitor Doctor

AFTER THE RETREAT from Concord and Lexington in April, 1775, and their hideous losses at Bunker Hill in June, the redcoats dared not venture out of Boston. They held the city, the harbor, and a few islands. Across the Charles River, in Cambridge, the Americans settled down to siege warfare.

Except for a little artillery fire, there was no fighting. Neither side could get at the other across the Charles River. In this deadlock each side had to know what the other was doing. Ordinary scouts and patrols could not do much. Never had spies been more sorely needed, and both sides had many. British General Gage's secret agents slipped out from Boston in various ways. Sometimes they rode or walked through the American camps, counting the soldiers when they fell in for daily prayers, examining the artillery, locating the various camps. One traitor-sergeant in the patriot forces kept up a correspondence with a redcoat British artillery sergeant in Boston. A blacksmith in the town of Mystic, near Cambridge, spied for Gage. One daring British spy crossed regularly on the Charles River ferry from Boston to talk with soldiers, and even one or two generals, on the American side.

American spies were just as active. The fishing schooners gave them a fine chance to slip in and out of Boston. When a patriot spy had finished his work in Boston, he simply went aboard a fishing schooner whose captain was also in the secret service. When the schooner was safely out of sight along the coast, the spy went ashore to make his report.

One day General Washington was shocked to see General Nathanael Greene looking very serious as he rode up to Craigie House on Brattle Street in Cambridge, where the American commander in chief had his headquarters. Gravely, Greene handed General Washington a paper.

Where did this come from? What did it mean?

General Greene had brought with him a baker from Newport, Rhode Island, who could tell where the letter came from. No one knew what it said; no one could read the queer writing. But everyone knew what it meant. It meant treason. The "writing" looked like this:

The baker, Godfrey Wenwood, had a strange tale to tell. Some years before, he had known a girl now living in Cambridge, but he hadn't seen her for a long time. In fact he was now engaged to another girl in Newport. His former girl friend had suddenly come to see him in his Newport bakery, carrying this very letter. She came to beg her former beau to introduce her to Captain Sir James Wallace, commanding H.M.S. *Rose*, then stationed at Newport.

There was something very odd about this, as the baker instantly realized. Why should this girl, whom he hadn't seen for some time, suddenly come and ask him to put her in touch with a senior naval officer—a naval officer of the enemy?

Wenwood did not like it. As he demurred and delayed, the girl chattered on.

Well, if he couldn't arrange a meeting for her with Captain Wallace, what about Mr. Charles Dudley? He'd do just as well. Now, Mr. Charles Dudley was the royal collector of customs. How did she know all these names? These British names!

The foolish girl was, by this time, no doubt rather enjoying herself because, seeing Godfrey's surprise or puzzlement, she rattled on: Well, if he couldn't arrange for her to meet either of these two gentlemen, surely he could introduce her to Mr. George Rome, a shipowner and merchant. He *must* know him.

He certainly did! Mr. Rome was a prominent Newport Tory. Moreover, being in the food business himself, the baker knew that George Rome was helping Captain Wallace supply the besieged British garrison in Boston.

Wenwood was not at all stupid. He did not like the sound of this. Besides, he wanted to get this girl out of town, and soon. Suppose his fiancée heard about her? He hemmed and hawed and asked questions. Why did she want to meet all these Tories? Finally the girl admitted that she had been given a letter in Cambridge which she was to deliver, by hand, to one of the three gentlemen she had named. Who gave her the letter? She wouldn't say. It was addressed to a British officer in Boston.—In Boston? Why had she come from Cambridge, where you could see Boston across the river, all the way to Newport, Rhode Island, to deliver it! What's more, the British officer to whom the letter was addressed was no ordinary officer. He was a staff officer of General Gage.

Fishy, thought Wenwood. Very fishy, indeed. What a crazy way of getting a letter from Cambridge to Boston!

Godfrey's persuasive powers were still good with his erstwhile sweetheart. He told her just to leave the letter with him. He would attend to it himself.

She consented, considered her errand accomplished, and departed for home.

After getting rid of her, Wenwood puzzled over the letter a while without opening it. Then he hunted up his friend Adam Maxwell, who had kept school the previous winter in the Brick Market, not far from the bakery. He knew Maxwell was a stanch patriot who could be trusted with this highly confidential story.

The schoolmaster did not hesitate. He broke the seal of the letter and found inside three pages closely scrawled over with mysterious characters.

Cipher! Here was something too secret to write in plain English! But instead of delivering this important piece of paper to an American army officer at once, Wenwood and Maxwell decided to put it away and do nothing.

August went by.

Late in September Godfrey Wenwood received a letter from the girl who had called on him in July. She was anxious to know why he had not sent "wot you promest to send." It had never been received. Now she begged him to come to Cambridge to see her and, also, to see " a certain person here" who wanted very much to see Wenwood.

This letter was like an electric shock. How did this girl know the letter had never reached the British staff officer in Boston? She must have contact with the British from Cambridge, the American side, where she lived! She must definitely be working for the enemy!

Wenwood consulted his friend Maxwell again. The two decided to do what they should have done two months before. They went to Henry Ward, patriot secretary of the Rhode Island colony. Mr. Ward told them to take the letter to Brigadier General Nathanael Greene, commanding the Rhode Island troops in Cambridge.

After one look at the mysterious pages, General Greene went to see the commander in chief privately. A glance at the ciphered pages told Washington there was something wrong. Here was treason. Orders rapped out swiftly. The girl was to be arrested at once and brought in for questioning.

That evening General Washington, standing at the front window, saw General Israel Putnam riding up the street with the girl on a pillion behind him. A pillion was a small second seat behind a horseman's saddle. Anyone riding it had to clasp the horseman tightly about the waist. The sight of tubby General Putnam riding down Brattle Street with the girl holding him tightly was funny enough to tickle Washington's sense of humor. Though he rarely laughed, and though the situation was serious, he burst into a roar.

By the time General Putnam and his fair young captive entered the front door, however, the commander in chief had wiped off the laugh and was deadly serious. Descending as far as the stair landing, he stood there, six feet tall, and glared sternly down. In his uniform of dark blue and buff, with three silver stars gleaming on gold epaulets, he made a magnificent and imposing figure.

Looking up at the commander in chief, the guilty girl heard him say that "nothing but a full confession could save her from the halter."

But she held out a long time against threats, persuasions, and endless questions:

What was in the letter?

She couldn't read it.

What was it about?

She didn't know.

Where was the cipher key?

How could she know the letter was ciphered? She hadn't opened it.

Who had given it to her?

She wouldn't tell!

The questions went on and on, perhaps all night. She was told that she had been carrying information to the enemy. Did she know what the penalty for that was? Her only chance was to tell everything. Finally exhaustion beat her down.

Dr. Benjamin Church had given her the letter, she said.

Her questioners were dumbfounded. What? Dr. Church? Impossible!

Dr. Church was a highly respected citizen, and one of the foremost medical men in all New England. He was the patriot's surgeon general. The commander in chief had complete faith in him.

Dr. Church had been attending the army's wounded. He had seen the fight at Lexington—so he said. He had long been a member of the Massachusetts Provincial Congress—had even been sent to Philadelphia to visit the Continental Congress. He knew everything the Americans were planning!

A graduate of Harvard, Church had gone to England to study medicine, had traveled in Europe, had married an English girl. Returning to settle in Boston, he had built an expensive summer house at which his neighbors marveled. He had written political verse in defense of the Whigs. (Some people noticed that these clever verses could easily be changed around in defense of the Tories!) Dr. Church had ridden to Springfield to greet Washington. How could one believe that the British had this trusted superpatriot (as he seemed) spying for them?

Though it was a fact that Paul Revere's spy ring in Boston had spotted some suspicious leaks, no one ever dreamed of connecting them with that esteemed citizen, Dr. Benjamin Church. Thinking back, however, people recalled that for a little while before the Revolution broke out, there were those who wondered whether Dr. Church was so wholeheartedly for the American cause as he professed. People could not help observing that the man loved luxury and spent a great deal of money; that there were times when he seemed to need money; and then times when he appeared to possess an unaccountable plenty of it.

When the girl at last pronounced Church's name, Washington knew he must talk to him at once. The doctor was easily found, quietly going about his medical duties, when the guard went after him. Bland, confident, almost convincing, he answered questions easily:

The letter?

Oh yes, it was his, he admitted smoothly. Why not? Many letters were being sent openly through the lines to Boston.

Perhaps so. But Church's letter was a little different. It had been kept secret. Why? It was in cipher. Why?

General Washington pointed out icily that if Dr. Church had wanted to send an innocent letter to Boston, he could have done so any time, under a flag of truce. Other Americans did. Why had he sent his letter, secretly, all the way around by way of Newport?

At this point Church mumbled that he had been indiscreet. But as for treason, he denied it.

Church was kept under guard, while three men who understood deciphering were put to work to "crack" the ciphered letter.

In the English language, letter frequencies run in about the order used on the modern linotype keyboard. *E* is the most frequently used letter in the alphabet. Today cryptographers (men

who analyze codes and ciphers) use two orders
of letter frequency:

ETOANIRSHDL·

or: ETOANRISHDL

Evidently the three men knew this principle.
They must have counted the number of times
each symbol occurred and arranged these in
order of frequency. They might also have noted
certain letter combinations that are common in
English, such as *ee, ng, th,* and so forth, which
would have given further clues.

Two independent analyses were made, one by
the Reverend Samuel West, working alone, the
other by Colonel Elisha Porter and Elbridge
Gerry, working together. By October 3, George
Washington received from them their two separate deciphers, showing what the letter said "in
clear." The two versions agreed. There could be
no doubt now.

In his letter Church had told the enemy all
about his recent visit to the Congress in Philadelphia (in June), adding that the mood of Congress was "determined in opposition." In other
words, he was informing the British that the
Americans would not back down. He gave them
a thorough report on American strength, artillery,
ammunition supply, rations, recruiting—everything an enemy would want to know. He even

gave the figures on the artillery at Kings Bridge, New York, which he had observed and counted! He gave the troop strength in Philadelphia. His letter also stated that he had tried three times before to send them information secretly. Once his messenger had been caught with the message sewed into the waistband of his breeches. But the captors did not find the message, and the man was released after a few days when Church himself had come to the rescue with a little cash and smooth talk. Church had sent the girl on the roundabout trip to Newport only after other ways had failed.

The day General Washington received the "clear" communication, he called a council of war and laid the incriminating message before his generals. The prisoner was called in.

Being shown his message "in clear" the traitorous doctor had to admit that it had been correctly deciphered. But he was still trying to bluff it out. His motives, he said, had been entirely patriotic! The Wenwood letter might seem suspicious, but he had written it only to frighten the British with an exaggerated account of American strength.

Such a defense made no impression on the American generals who heard it, and the doctor was marched off to confinement, while his punishment was being considered.

To their astonishment, the American generals

now discovered that their Continental Congress had made a dreadful mistake. It had, it is true, adopted army regulations. But these early patriots didn't know very much about writing such regulations. They forbade communicating with the enemy—in other words, espionage. Anyone who did it could be court-martialed—that included Dr. Church! So far, so good.

But when the generals looked to see what sentence they could give him, they found that the Continental Congress, when it came to listing the penalties a court-martial could inflict, had forgotten all about possible spies. Church had betrayed his country for many months. He was a spy, and ought to have been hanged. But all a court-martial could do was fine him two months' pay, give him thirty-nine lashes, or dismiss him from the army! There was no legal way to hang Dr. Church, which was a great disappointment to everybody but the doctor.

Congress hastily authorized the death penalty for future spies, but as the law was not passed until the following month—November, 1775—it could not be applied to Church. All General Washington could do was hold the traitor in custody and try to seize his papers. But it was already too late. Another quick and clever British spy, who was never discovered, had already searched Church's papers and removed any incriminating evidence. Even his cipher key, which must have been in those papers, could not be found. Only a doctor's ordinary records were in his files.

Eventually Congress ordered Church kept in prison under severe restrictions. His windows were boarded up; he was not allowed to have pen, ink, and paper; he could speak to no one but the jailer.

After a short time the wretched prisoner was given writing materials just long enough for him to write, in January, 1776, an appeal to Congress. In this he complained that the severity of his confinement had brought on asthma and threatened his life. What he needed was clear air. Congress allowed him to be moved to another jail. He was not set free, since it was soon apparent that indignant patriots would lynch him if they got their hands on him. When his jail was raided, Church saved his life only by jumping out of a window. He was soon caught and back in jail.

The traitor was now hated so generally that a mob broke into his house and destroyed everything in it. His wife complained that they had not left her even a change of clothes, not even a bed for herself and her children to lie on. Eventually she found enough money to pay for passage back to England.

In 1780, Congress exiled Dr. Church, after

several years in prison, to an island in the West Indies and threatened him with death should he ever return.

He sailed on a small schooner, and nothing was ever heard of Church or the schooner again.

George Washington was horrified when he learned how closely the farseeing eye of British intelligence had been watching him. Even then he never guessed how long Dr. Church had been spying for the enemy, how much he had reported, nor how many other secret agents were working for British General Gage by watching and reporting all the patriots' early preparations for the revolutionary struggle.

Such secrets are rarely discovered until long after wars are over, when someone searches through the files that have come into the possession of the winning side. The full extent of Church's treason would be a secret even today, were it not for a casual remark in a letter to General Gage which definitely proves that Church was the author of a long series of intelligence reports. These are now with the Gage papers in the Clements Library at the University of Michigan.

Gage received this letter in the latter part of May, 1775. It was full of military information about the new American fortifications outside of Cambridge. Then the writer added that he had been appointed to carry dispatches to Philadelphia. Dr. Church *did* receive such an appointment in the middle of that month, and no one else received any similar appointment! So the traitorous Church was the author of this letter, too.

Not until Benedict Arnold's treason three years later did the British have the services of a turncoat so high in the scale of American leadership and so close to the heart of the patriots' plans.

Plots Within Plots

THE BRITISH REDCOATS in Boston just sat there, besieged, for almost a year. Finally, in March, 1776, about eleven months after the clashes at Lexington and Concord, General William Howe moved out. The American troops entered a little hesitantly, since they could see, still at their posts, British sentries—which turned out to be nothing but dummies dressed in scarlet coats!

At first the enemy army didn't go far. For days their ships lay at anchor, just off Boston. General Washington was puzzled, annoyed, suspicious. Why didn't they go? Were they playing a trick? Were they planning some kind of surprise?

"The enemy have the best knack at puzzling

people I ever met with in my life," said General Washington.

The obvious point for the next attack was New York City, and Washington started his riflemen and five infantry regiments thither at once. But was it safe to send more men away from Boston while the British fleet was still hanging around?

General Washington had something else to worry about: "There is one evil that I dread, and that is their spies." To deal with them, he ordered "a dozen or more of honest, sensible, and diligent men to haunt the communication between Roxbury and the different landing places nearest the shipping, in order to question all unknown persons."

At last a signal fluttered from the enemy flagship. White sails spread. The fleet moved out to sea and turned—south toward New York? No, north! They were going to Halifax.

The British army badly needed a chance to rest and reorganize. For that purpose General William Howe (who had succeeded General Gage in command) withdrew the whole force to Halifax. Meantime, to make sure of being ready in New York should the British decide to go there, Washington hurried his army down the coast and began to fortify the city.

While this was going on, a man named Henry

Dawkins got out of jail in New York City. Nobody now can tell why Henry Dawkins had been sent to jail in the first place, nor how long he had been there. Whatever the reason for sending him there, it was probably a good one. The man had hardly gotten out of jail after that first sentence before he was back again.

Few people now alive have ever heard of Henry Dawkins, though he was, in his time, a prominent engraver. He made bookplates, maps, caricatures, coats of arms, seal rings, and seals for the Philadelphia gentry. If he had stopped with that, everything would have been all right. The trouble was, Henry also began to engrave counterfeit money. He may have been making it for some time before 1776. No one really knows just how long he had been counterfeiting in Pennsylvania before he was caught and jailed in New York. But now he had served his sentence—whatever offense he had committed—and had been released.

Stirring matters were afoot as Henry Dawkins made his way from jail in New York City to Long Island in the spring of 1776. General Howe, in Halifax, was nearly ready to go back to war. Before long he would try to capture New York. In England a mighty fleet was preparing to sail for New York. It would bring fresh British troops and German mercenaries to strengthen the army that had failed in Boston.

Just off the New York and New Jersey coast, aboard H.M.S. *Duchess of Gordon,* hovered New York's royal governor, William Tryon. He had had to flee from the city. Now, safe aboard the king's man-o'-war, he was busily plotting with the Tories, who swarmed everywhere—in the city, on Long Island, and far up the Hudson Valley. Meantime his spies and secret couriers hurried back and forth.

The Tories were plotting the speedy capture or death of George Washington, the defeat of the Continental Army, the collapse of the American Revolution.

Henry Dawkins was the man who ruined all these Tory plans. Henry Dawkins saved the United States—and it was all by accident. He never meant to do it. He never knew he had done it. But he saved his country all the same.

Unaware that the destiny of a continent rode with him, Henry Dawkins was quietly enjoying his new-found freedom. It was springtime, and he proceeded at leisure through Long Island's country lanes to Huntington. His thoughts were upon neither the fate of nations nor the movements of armies. Dawkins was thinking up a new and interesting scheme whereby he could turn a dishonest shilling and a dishonest dollar at the same time. For Henry Dawkins, eager to "get rich quick," had no time to think about the state of his country. All he cared about was the state of Henry Dawkins.

After settling down at the home of the brothers Israel and Isaac Youngs in Huntington, Long Island, he asked Israel Youngs to help him buy a printing press. Dawkins was very insistent it should be what was then called a "rolling press." He felt sure, he said, that he could work up a profitable little printing business. What would he print? Well, there might be a tidy profit in printing labels to paste inside the hats which the local hat industry was producing.

Israel Youngs, to judge from the way he talked after his arrest, was a singularly unsuspicious person. He had no idea, he later protested with much emphasis, that a rolling press was used to print engravings. It never occurred to him that currency issued by Congress and the new state government was engraved. Oh no. But he did say, under considerable pressure, the thought had just once crossed his mind that something might be wrong about Dawkins. He had thought it a little odd when Dawkins signed his order for the new press with a fictitious name. But Israel Youngs saw no evil, heard no evil, spoke no evil—not when there was easy money in being blind, deaf, and dumb.

Even when, a little later, Dawkins installed his press in the attic (where there was no floor and where he had to lay boards across the beams) the unsuspicious Youngs brothers still asked no questions. They did admit it had seemed strange when Dawkins concealed the door to the attic!

After the press arrived, Dawkins remarked to Israel Youngs that he could make as good money as anybody else. When Israel repeated this remark to his smug brother, Isaac primly replied, "If he could, it would be a sin." Or so Israel later told the American officials.

Counterfeiting in those days was not very difficult. The crude currency of the new American states lacked the many protective devices of modern bank notes. It could easily be imitated. The provincial treasuries did know enough about currency to use a special kind of paper, but—alas for them—any printer could buy the same paper! To get some, the Dawkins counterfeiting ring turned to one Isaac Ketcham. And through Ketcham the original counterfeiting scheme became mixed up with Governor Tryon's plot to kill or kidnap Washington, crush the Continental Army, and capture New York City.

Money of that period was printed from several plates at a time, in large sheets, several notes to a sheet. After that the individual notes were cut apart. Any printer could cut a sample of the paper from the space between the notes. Carrying such a specimen, Ketcham went to Philadelphia—then a center of the American paper industry—and asked for prices. In ordinary times Ketcham's inquiries might have gone unnoticed, but these were not ordinary times. Someone suspected (correctly) a plot to counterfeit. About May of 1776 Ketcham was arrested. About the same time Dawkins got drunk. He made several rash remarks. These betrayed the counterfeiting plot. Then Dawkins, too, was arrested.

So far Dawkins, Ketcham, and the Youngs brothers, who presently joined them in jail, were guilty of nothing worse than attempted counterfeiting. But in the jail with them were other criminals, far worse than the counterfeiting ring: men who had engaged in treason against their country. These convicted traitors talked incautiously of Governor Tryon's Tory plots. Isaac Ketcham listened. He saw a chance to save himself. (He would also save his country. But that, to Ketcham, was incidental.)

This fantastic sequel to the counterfeiting scheme is one of the ironies of American history: Dawkins involved the Youngs brothers and Ketcham in counterfeiting. This scheme sent all four to jail. There Ketcham, at least, learned of Tory plots which, if successful, would have destroyed the new American army. With no motive higher than to save his own skin, Ketcham began to act as a "stool pigeon" in the jail. As a result, the Tory plots against General Washington and the Continental Army were discovered!

Enough of their secrets leaked out to show that the Tories had at least two dangerous plans. The first plan was to kidnap George Washington from his New York headquarters, together with as many men of his guard as could be captured. This was admitted in London after the Revolution was over, by ringleader David Matthews, the former Tory mayor of New York.

The second plot was for a sudden uprising of armed Tories. This was to take place *behind* the American army in Manhattan, on Long Island, and also along the Hudson River as far north as the Highlands, near West Point. It was to be timed so that General Howe's soldiers and the ships commanded by his brother, Admiral Lord Howe, would be attacking the American front together. At the same time the Tory partisans planned to blow up American powder magazines, seize all American artillery, and shell the American army from behind, with its own guns. King's Bridge was to be cut, so that the patriots would have no chance of escaping from Manhattan into Westchester County. Some of the plotters themselves confessed these plans after the Americans caught them.

Fantastic though these schemes may sound today, they had a fair chance of success. Strong and secret Tory forces were already well organized and prepared to go into action. One band of seven hundred king's men was ready to rise on Long Island. There was another, almost as large, at Goshen, New York. Tories at Cornwall were ready to raid the new American fortifications in the Highlands and to spike their cannon. These Tory guerrilla bands were steadily increasing in number. British recruiting agents were moving secretly through the American lines into New York City, upstate New York, New Jersey, and Connecticut, organizing more and more secret companies of king's militia.

The king's men had the further advantage of a wide-ranging system of spies and secret couriers, which had been established in and around New York almost as soon as hostilities began. The Tory governor of New York, William Tryon, aboard the British ship *Duchess of Gordon,* Captain Vandeput aboard the *Asia,* and Captain Wallace aboard the *Rose* could move about the coast as they pleased. There was no American navy to chase them off. Boats could put off from shore at any time, bringing aboard Tory recruits, spies, information, arms, or supplies. British couriers and secret agents could land anywhere along Long Island or the Jersey coast. The enemy's secret communication was perfect. British agents also had corrupted several soldiers of Washington's guard. The plotters were installed in two New York taverns. Under such conditions the plots to kidnap Washington and to attack the American rear seemed almost certain of success.

Then suddenly things went wrong. According to New York City's Tory mayor, David Matthews, the plot to kidnap Washington failed because of "an unfortunate Discovery that was made of a Letter." Others said that some of his conspirators, talking indiscreetly about their plans, were overheard by a patriotic waiter, William Corbie. It was Corbie, so the story went, who informed Joseph Smith, a prominent citizen, who took immediate action to have Mayor Matthews and his co-plotters arrested. But the official records show that it was really Dawkins who, by landing his fellow counterfeiters in jail, started the train of events that wrecked the plot against General Washington.

It is not known whether Dawkins himself and the Youngs brothers ever heard about the Tory plots, but Ketcham, soon after he had been confined, got wind of the conspiracies from gossip among the prisoners. Could he escape punishment for counterfeiting, he wondered, by revealing treason?

In early June of 1776 Ketcham sent a petition to the Provincial Congress. He now felt shame "for his past Misconduct." He told a sad tale about "six poor Children," and begged to be let out on bail to take care of them. At the end of his petition he added, as if it were a mere afterthought, that he had something else to tell. It was not about his own imprisonment, he explained, but entirely on another matter.

The speaker of the Provincial Congress let Ketcham out of jail long enough to explain what he meant. What was the other subject? That subject was, of course, the series of Tory plots. Later someone wrote at the bottom of Ketcham's petition: "The application of Isaac Ketcham and the memorandum which finally ended in the execution of Thomas Hickey for high treason."

Ketcham began his revelations by showing that there were several traitors within Washington's bodyguard. As soon as the amazed speaker heard this first story, he promised Ketcham a pardon if he would go back to jail for a while and act as an American spy. Ketcham was only too glad to escape punishment in any way he could.

He soon had a great deal more information, all centering around one Thomas Hickey.

But who was Thomas Hickey? He was one of two new prisoners, arrested June 15, 1776, who had arrived in the same jail as Ketcham and the other counterfeiters. Both had been members of General Washington's guard, a specially picked group of American soldiers. One was Sergeant Thomas Hickey, and the other Private Michael Lynch. They too had been caught passing counterfeit money. If they had both kept quiet, there would never have been any worse charges against them. The Tory uprisings might have taken place as planned, and the attempt to kidnap Washington might have succeeded. Complete disaster would have befallen the thirteen colonies, and the American Revolution would have ended then and there.

But Hickey foolishly boasted of being deep in Tory plots. Ketcham listened quietly. Then he pumped Hickey, and also Lynch. He learned all about their schemes. Soon he was able to send word to the Provincial Congress; both men were involved in the treason he had already hinted at.

Just then further alarming news reached the patriots, and confirmed Ketcham's report. A patriotic businessman named William Leary happened to meet a former employee, James Mason. Mason confided that he and some others were in British pay. Leary informed the authorities, who arrested Mason. Under questioning, Mason also implicated Thomas Hickey. He gave the names of others: Gilbert Forbes, a Broadway gunsmith, William Green, a drummer in the guard, James Johnson, a fifer, a soldier in the guard named Barnes, and another Forbes, whose first name was William. Both Leary and Mason implicated the Tory mayor, David Matthews, who had long been under suspicion, and who had contributed £100 for the expenses of the plot.

Arrests came swiftly. Hickey was already in jail when Ketcham and Mason implicated him in treason. Mayor David Matthews was seized at his Flatbush home at one o'clock in the morning of June 22. Gilbert Forbes was arrested about the same hour. Green, Johnson, and Barnes of the bodyguard were arrested. Some Tories took to the woods and escaped. In all, twenty or more were arrested.

As usual in wartime, the wildest rumors began to spread. The story went round that Hickey had poisoned a dish of green peas (of which Washington was specially fond), but that his housekeeper warned Washington in time to send the peas away untasted. People said that when someone threw the peas out to the chickens, they all died!

Sergeant Hickey went before a court-martial,

charged with "exciting and joining in a mutiny and sedition, and of treacherously corresponding with, enlisting among, and receiving pay from the enemies of the United *American* Colonies." Since these charges were enough to hang any soldier, nothing was said about kidnaping or assassinating the commander in chief, or passing counterfeit money. Though Hickey pleaded not guilty, there was never any hope for him.

After hearing all the witnesses and Hickey's pitiably weak defense, the court-martial's verdict was unanimous: "That the prisoner, Thomas Hickey, suffer death for said crimes by being hanged by the neck till he is dead." None of the other plotters was brought to trial. No one knows why. Perhaps they secretly gave information the Americans could use. No one knows what became of any of them except Mayor Matthews, who eventually reached England with other Tories.

Hickey was offered religious advice from a chaplain. Hickey didn't like chaplains. He snarled that they were "all Cut throats." Then somebody started to put up a gallows near the Bowery, in New York City. The execution was fixed for eleven o'clock on the morning of June 28.

On Hickey's last morning the brigades of Generals Heath, Scott, Spencer, and Lord Stirling (a patriot officer even though he claimed to be a lord) were ordered to parade at ten o'clock

and march to the place of execution. Eighty men
—twenty from each brigade, "with good Arms
and Bayonets"—were ordered out as a guard for
the unfortunate Hickey on his last mile. There
had been so much plotting already that great
care was taken against a possible attempt at rescue. In all, about twenty thousand people
gathered there to watch the traitor die.

Hickey was sullen as he stood at the gallows
that warm, sunny day in June. It is an awful
thing to die for wrongdoing when one is young,
when summer is just beginning, when life seems
so attractive. Hickey had been ungracious when
offered the consolation of the clergy, but a chaplain did go with him to the end. Though Hickey
appeared obstinate and unmoved almost to the
last, a torrent of tears flowed over his face when
the chaplain took him by the hand to say good-
bye. He wiped them away with his hand. On
went the noose and blindfold. Hickey swung off
into the air, writhed for a few dreadful minutes,
and then hung limp.

General Washington drove home the moral
of the ghastly spectacle his court-martial had
provided. Orders for the day said:

The unhappy fate of *Thomas Hickey*, ex-
ecuted this day for mutiny, sedition, and

treachery, the General hopes will be a warning to every soldier in the Army to avoid those crimes, and all others, so disgraceful to the character of a soldier, and pernicious to his country, whose pay he receives and bread he eats.

The conspiracies had been detected just in time. General Howe's personal transport had been lying in New York Harbor for three days when Sergeant Thomas Hickey swung from the gallows. American alarm flags were flying on Staten Island. British ships were beginning to crowd each other in the bay till their masts resembled a forest. Howe's attack was coming. But the Americans no longer feared a second attack from the rear, nor the kidnaping of their commander.

As a reward, Ketcham was set free. In a sense, however, the Continental Army owed all this to Henry Dawkins. And where was he? Back in jail again!

Nathan Hale

A Hero Wasted

Two days after British spy Thomas Hickey dangled at the end of a rope, General Howe began to land his redcoats on Staten Island (June 30, 1776). General Washington had to let them come ashore unresisted. There was nothing else to do. He simply hadn't men enough to hold Staten Island as well as Manhattan. Two weeks later Admiral Lord Howe, the general's brother, came sailing into New York Harbor with a powerful fleet and more troops, both British and German. Two weeks after that, General Sir Henry Clinton, having been thoroughly defeated at Charleston, South Carolina, brought his redcoats back to aid Howe's attack on New York. British power was concentrating.

Though it was clearly impossible for the Americans to defend Manhattan Island and Long Island for any length of time against a hostile army and navy, Congress insisted the attempt be made. Always the well-disciplined soldier, General Washington obediently undertook the hopeless task.

Now was the time for the patriots to set up a good intelligence net like the one Revere and his friends had set up in Massachusetts. Men should have been found to serve as spies on Staten Island. An espionage network should then have been established secretly on Manhattan and Long Island. They would not be needed so long as Americans were there, but they would be all ready to begin spying for Washington as soon as he was forced to withdraw. Everyone knew he would surely have to give up New York sooner or later.

Though such a network could have kept General Washington fully informed, no one thought of it in time. One or two patriot spies, probably volunteers, did remain on Staten Island, but they had no way of sending their information when they got it. Secret agents are of no help at all if they cannot send their intelligence to the generals who can use it. Secret couriers, therefore, were as much needed as spies.

Two days after the British won the Battle of

Long Island on August 27, 1776, General Washington had to pull his forces away from Brooklyn to Manhattan. Now the great commander needed an organized channel of information more than ever. It was of the utmost importance to find out ahead of time what Sir William Howe was going to do. Three days later Washington was urging General Heath and General George Clinton to set up a new espionage network. He hoped that Clinton, as a New Yorker, might be able to find volunteer spies "in whom a confidence may be reposed." If no patriots willing to do such work could be found, perhaps some Tory might be bribed to spy "for a reasonable reward."

Within a few days the worried commander in chief needed information so badly that he did not care whether the reward was reasonable or not. He wrote his generals again. They were to stick at no expense. Washington simply had to find out about the enemy. "I was never more uneasy than on account of my want of knowledge," he wrote.

As precious days went by with no information coming in, there was only one thing left for General Washington to do: he would have to send a spy into the British lines on Long Island.

A more experienced intelligence service than the Americans yet possessed would have sent in several agents, in case one was caught. Instead, General Washington asked Lieutenant Colonel Thomas Knowlton to find a solitary volunteer. Knowlton asked Lieutenant James Sprague, a veteran of the French and Indian War, to undertake the dangerous task. No soldier is ever *ordered* to become a spy. He is simply asked to volunteer. Sprague had a right to refuse, and did so. "I am willing," said he, "to go & fight them, but as for going among them & being taken & hung up like a dog, I will not do it."

The lieutenant colonel then called a meeting of all the officers of Knowlton's Rangers and put the question to them. No one liked the idea. Just as it appeared that no one at all would volunteer, there was a sudden stir at the door. Captain Nathan Hale, still white from a recent illness, joined the group.

"I will undertake it," he said.

The volunteer, a young Yale athlete of the class of 1773, now a schoolmaster at Haddam, Connecticut, had joined Webb's Connecticut Regiment at the outbreak of the Revolution. Later he had transferred to Knowlton's Rangers. An ardent patriot, he was impelled to volunteer to be a spy solely by a sense of duty. There would be no prospect of glory. (Who sings the praises of an agent, whose work must all be secret?) There would be constant danger. There would be the risk of death upon the gallows.

American intelligence planned Hale's dangerous mission about as badly as it could be planned. In the first place, though he was brave, loyal, and well educated, Nathan Hale was the wrong man for the job. Anyone who had ever seen him was certain to recognize him. Disguise was of little use. Not only was he tall, sturdy, and handsome, he was also literally a marked man. His face had been scarred by exploding powder. Worse still, his Tory cousin, Samuel Hale, was at that very moment serving with the British.

Hale was given no training, no planned cover, no contact with patriotic American civilians living within the British lines. No line of communication was arranged. He was given no code, no cipher, no signal system, and no secret ink, though an American doctor had invented a formula for it three years earlier. Having run the first hideous risk of collecting information, Hale would have to carry about with him his own written notes. If he were caught, the notes would instantly prove him a spy.

Neither was enough care taken to maintain secrecy about Hale's mission. He should never have been allowed to volunteer in front of a group of other officers. After that, every officer in Knowlton's Rangers knew Hale was going out as a spy. When their captain disappeared suddenly, all his men were certain to wonder where he was and talk about it. False orders should have been issued to conceal what Hale was really doing. No one thought of it. Though all these men were loyal Americans, loyalty is not the same as silence. Gossip by the campfires might be overheard by any British spy who happened to be around.

General Washington soon learned to manage his espionage better than this. Later in the war, secret agents he sent in to the British were carefully coached and given cover. As a result, most of them came safely back. But that was no help to Nathan Hale!

Worst of all, Captain Hale, who had had no experience in military intelligence at all, was not cautioned to maintain silence himself. Before starting, he talked the whole plan over with his friend, Captain William Hull, a Yale classmate who had been a brother officer in Webb's Regiment before Hale transferred to the Rangers. Hull was perfectly loyal too, but a spy ought never discuss his secret mission with anyone except the officer who sends him out.

Horrified to learn what his brother officer meant to do, Hull tried hard to dissuade him, but Hale was determined. He felt it was his duty to get the information so desperately needed by the commander of his country's armies.

Hull reminded the brave young officer that, though Hale viewed the business of a spy as a duty, yet he could not officially be required to perform it. "Such a service is not demanded of the meanest soldier." Captain Hull added, "Besides, your nature is too frank and open for deceit and disguise." There was also the disgraceful nature of espionage.

"Who," asked Hull, "respects the character of a spy?"

The conscientious Hale answered, "For a year I have been attached to the army, and have not rendered any material service." As for the supposed disgrace of espionage, the noble young captain said, "Every kind of service, necessary to the public good, becomes honorable by being necessary."

That was the last time Hull ever saw his friend. Hale simply disappeared. But the gallant spy's next movements can be accurately traced, because he took with him Sergeant Stephen Hempstead, who later published the whole story. Hale had been provided with a general order to all American armed vessels to take him any place he wanted to go. He told Sergeant Hempstead to come with him as far as he could in safety, and to wait there for his return.

They left Harlem Heights, on the upper half of Manhattan Island, on or about September 12, 1776. Going from New York State into Connecticut, they started looking for a safe place to cross Long Island Sound. This proved impossible near New York City, because the coast there was guarded by British naval vessels. Their small tenders could row inshore and block any passage. The captain and the sergeant could find no way to cross until, at Norwalk, they came upon the armed American sloop *Schuyler*, commanded by Captain Charles Pond.

Thus far Nathan Hale had remained in uniform—though not the colonial buff and dark blue with epaulets, which only Washington and a few senior officers owned. Hale wore a "frock" —not a coat, but a long hunting shirt—made of white linen, and fringed. It was the kind of thing that American officers wore for field service. He had with him, however, "a plain suit of citizen's brown clothes."

Since he had had two years' experience in school teaching, he assumed the character of a schoolmaster. He would pretend to be looking for a school. This made a plausible story, since in September an unemployed teacher would nat-

urally be doing just that. Hale carried his Yale
diploma with him. It would help his pose as a
teacher, which, in fact, he was. The diploma had
his name on it. He had to trust to luck that the
British would not know the name of such a
junior officer. He was shrewd enough to leave
his silver shoe buckles with Sergeant Hempstead.
They would not comport with his character of
schoolmaster, he said.

Taking him across Long Island Sound, the
schooner dropped him at Huntington, Long
Island, where American secret missions continued
to slip in during the rest of the war. From the
moment Captain Pond put him ashore until his
capture, Hale's movements are veiled in mystery.
This is not remarkable. Hale was on a secret mission in enemy-held territory. His papers disappeared. His captors hanged him without trial.
In the absence of a court-martial record, all that
we know is what Captain John Montresor, chief
engineer of the British army, told the American
officers who received him under a flag of truce
the evening after Hale had been hanged. Montresor, who had seen Nathan Hale just before
his execution, said he had passed through the
British army lines both on Long Island and in
New York City. He had made sketches of their
fortifications and memoranda of their number

and dispositions. It was exactly what General
Washington wanted, but alas, the fearless spy
was never able to deliver his intelligence.

Hale had hardly reached Long Island when the
military situation changed entirely. On September 15, 1776, the British seized Manhattan. After
that, British positions on Long Island were no
longer important to Washington. A less devoted
spy might simply have returned, but the conscientious Hale went boldly on to Manhattan
to observe the new positions of the enemy. He
knew that was the information Washington now
needed.

By the time he reached New York City, the
Americans had been pushed back to about where
127th Street now runs. The British held the 106th
Street line, with advanced posts as far north as
110th Street or beyond; and there was some
vigorous skirmishing between the lines, in which,
for the first time, American troops, fighting in
the open field and without entrenchments, put
the redcoats to flight.

By September 21 the disguised American captain was back in upper Manhattan, from where
he had started with Sergeant Hempstead. By
this time he had been in enemy-held territory
more than a week, in danger of being recognized
at every instant. It has been said that he pushed
northward till he reached the British front, where

of course the most valuable information was to be found. If so, he passed through—and observed —Lord Percy's troops, lying in reserve somewhere near the eastern part of Eightieth Street; Sir Henry Clinton's troops, along a line not far from Ninety-third Street; and Lord Cornwallis' troops, whose main line of resistance was near 106th Street. He had certainly seen all the field fortifications the British had erected. He thus had all the information General Washington needed.

From the British front, the secret agent could look across—and safely to the American outposts on the high ground not far north of 127th Street. His problem now was how to return. Captain Hale could not cross the front openly, but he may have hoped to row a boat around the flanks of both armies and land safely in the American rear. Or he may have hoped to slip through no man's land, around what is now Columbia University, and back to the Continental Army.

Since Sergeant Hempstead had been ordered to wait for him at Norwalk, the original plan must have been to send a small boat to pick Hale up on the north shore of Long Island. But now, the military situation had completely changed in the past week; it would be extremely dangerous now for the spy to return to Long

Island. The planned escape route there was useless.

Sometime during the night of September 21 Hale was arrested. As explained earlier, he was hanged almost at once, without trial, and no one (except his captors) has ever known just what happened. There were several stories. Probably the true one is that Hale was caught because he mistook a small boat from a British warship for an American craft.

According to this story, Washington's secret agent was captured by sailors from the British ship *Halifax,* lying off Whitestone Point. The captain of the ship, William Quarme, went ashore in a small boat, near the foot of 111th Street. Hale saw the boat coming in. In daylight he would have seen the British uniforms, but it was dark and he approached the boat before he saw his mistake. Hale had no reason to suppose that a boat from the American forces would put in here to take him off, but he may have thought that the little craft contained American civilians from Long Island, who would take him across the East River.

When he saw his mistake, he is said to have shown agitation. Even without this, Captain Quarme would naturally have been suspicious. There was something very queer about a civilian schoolmaster so near the front.

His men seized Hale and turned him over to the army. After that, the main outline of the final tragedy is clear. In addition to the account given by the British army's chief engineer, Captain Montresor, several British officers' diaries mention the affair. General Howe had set up his headquarters in the house of James Beekman, on the East River at the corner of First Avenue and Fifty-first Street, now called Beekman Place. Being under suspicion, Hale must have been searched before he was taken to the commanding general. The incriminating papers that he carried must have been found at once.

The prisoner admitted that he was an American officer in disguise. After that, General Howe ordered him hanged, without trial. This hasty condemnation does not show the British general in a good light. However, a British officer says the usually good-natured British general regretted Hale's fate. Hale's "manly bearing and the evident disinterested patriotism of the handsome young prisoner sensibly touched a chord of General Howe's nature; but the stern rules of war concerning such offenses would not allow him to exercise even pity."

Once Howe had ordered the execution, his prisoner passed into the custody of William Cunningham, provost marshal of the British forces. Hale was confined for the night in the Beekman greenhouse, adjoining the mansion. As he was to die in the morning, it was not worth while taking him four miles down Manhattan Island to the city jail.

Captain John Montresor, a British engineer officer who entered the American lines under a flag of truce soon after, told the story of the hanging to Captain Alexander Hamilton, of the American artillery, and Captain William Hull, Hale's friend in Webb's Regiment. Hull recorded: "I learned the melanchcly particulars from this officer, who was present at his execution, and seemed touched by the circumstances attending it."

Even though he was himself a British officer, Captain Montresor described Cunningham as "hardened to human suffering and every softening sentiment of the heart." He said that Hale had asked for a clergyman. He was refused. He then requested a Bible; that too was refused. Captain Montresor's statements must have been accurate, for he had no reason to blacken the character of his own army's provost in talking with enemy officers. He himself appears to have reached the American camp indignant at what he had witnessed that very morning. (Somehow, we are not sorry to learn that Cunningham himself was hanged for forgery in London, several years after the war.)

There was a delay after Hale was brought to the gallows at the artillery park, where Captain Montresor had his tent. Pitying the condemned man, the sympathetic Montresor asked the provost marshal (Cunningham) to permit the prisoner to sit there while preparations were being made. "Captain Hale entered; he was calm, and bore himself with gentle dignity, in the consciousness of rectitude and high intentions," Montresor reported. "He asked for writing materials, which I furnished him: he wrote two letters."

Without quoting Montresor further, Hale's friend Hull wrote down the rest of the ghastly story in his own words: "He was shortly summoned to the gallows. But a few persons were around him, yet his characteristic dying words were remembered. He said, "I only regret that I have but one life to lose for my country."

These famous dying words are thus fully authenticated. Montresor had heard them only a few hours earlier when he repeated them to the Americans, Hull and Hamilton. They were, in fact, derived from a line in Joseph Addison's *Cato*:

> What pity is it
> That we can die but once to serve our country!

The play was much read by educated Americans, and was often in the mind of Washington, whose writing frequently quoted paraphrased passages from it. Hale's eager reading and his activity in the Linonian Society as a Yale undergraduate all indicate a knowledge of the English classics. In fact, there still exists a letter written to him by a girl with whom he corresponded, quoting from *Cato*.

The patriotic Nathan Hale had gone to war quoting a tag from Horace: *Dulce et decorum est pro patria mori.* ("Sweet and fitting is death for one's country.") So his career as an American soldier began and ended in the same mood, each time with a quotation from the classics, as befitted a scholar in arms.

Hale handed his farewell letters to Montresor, who must have passed them over, however reluctantly, to Cunningham, instead of bringing them across the lines later in the day.

About three months after Hale's death, Major John Wyllys, who had been captured September 15 during the American retreat from New York, was exchanged. The Reverend Enoch Hale rode to Wethersfield, Connecticut, to see him and inquire about his brother's death. Being himself in jail, Wyllys had not seen Nathan Hale, but he had spoken with Cunningham soon after the hanging. Enoch Hale recorded in his diary: "He saw my Brother's Diploma which the Provost

Marshal showed him who also had two letters of his—one to me, the other to his commanding officer written after he was sentenced."

Probably Captain William Hull was right when he wrote that the provost "in a diabolical spirit of cruelty, destroyed the letters of the prisoner, and assigned as a reason that the rebels should never know they had a man who could die with so much firmness."

Thus did Nathan Hale, schoolteacher, become an example of soldierly courage and nobility of character, as well as a great American hero.

If the British thought that the hanging of Hale would deter other patriots from attempting these dangerous missions, they were mistaken. A spy named Joshua Davis (who would later assist the successful Culper ring of American spies on Manhattan and Long Island) entered the British lines almost immediately, returned safely, and was paid for his mission on September 29, just a week after the death of Nathan Hale.

Spiderweb of Spies

AFTER HOWE'S ARMY OF REDCOATS had occupied New York City, the secret services of both sides became more active and also more efficient. American secret agents soon were able to enter New York City, secure a certain amount of military intelligence, and then slip safely out again. The British began to have more success in catching American spies and to receive a good deal of valuable information from their own.

At first both sides learned a good deal simply by quizzing ordinary travelers. Amazing as it seems today, each army allowed travelers on private business to go back and forth across the lines. It was a dangerous freedom. British officers, well aware how much information refugees and temporary visitors brought with them, picked people up for questioning as soon as they reached New York. But since the British usually let them go home again, they carried nearly as much information back to the Americans as they had given the British.

The most important military secret the Americans learned in this way was the British plan for General Burgoyne's intended march south from Canada through Ticonderoga and down the Hudson Valley. If Burgoyne could join other British forces somewhere near Albany, the redcoats would cut the thirteen colonies in two. The American spy who revealed this whole scheme made his report to the New York State Commission on Conspiracies thirteen days before Burgoyne submitted his written plan to the King in London! The American spy must have heard British officers discussing war plans before General Burgoyne sailed for England!

It was not enough for the American spies to find out what the British meant to do. They also had to try to spot the Tories who were still living in their usual homes, behind the American lines or right with the American forces. Many of these people were likely to be British spies. The Americans also made every effort to keep the Tories from forming militia companies. Tory leaders organized these in territory which the

Americans held. Then, when each company was complete, it slipped off to reinforce the redcoats in New York. All this went hand in hand with British espionage.

Washington did everything in his power to block the channels of secret communication, which he knew British spies were using. It was very hard to find them, but before long the Americans were catching a good many of the enemy's secret agents, though some were dressed in fantastic disguises. One was caught in women's clothes, "trying to go above the ferry." Another British spy captured by the Americans had disguised even his horse!

A good many other British agents were caught and punished, usually by death. When, in April, 1777, American militia surrounded and searched the house of John Hunt at White Plains, New York, they found first "some Oranges, Tea & some Buckles," then a man hiding between a straw mattress and a featherbed. Tea and oranges were imported only by the British! And why should an innocent man be between a mattress and a featherbed—hardly a comfortable spot! Searching further, the Americans found, in a back room, another man, Simon Mabie. He was carrying a warrant issued by General William Howe, authorizing him to recruit Tories. This was dated March 30, 1777, only a few days earlier. Mabie also had a certificate stating he was loyal to the king. Taken before a court-martial, he admitted enlisting soldiers for the royal forces. He too was sentenced to be hanged.

Not all sentences were so severe. Sometimes Tory prisoners were sentenced to imprisonment for a year, six months, or three months, or fined as little as fifteen dollars. Sometimes Tories were branded with a hot iron in the form of the letter *T*—a form of punishment long used in England.

Sometimes the Americans knew very well that spies were lurking about but could not catch them. For instance, in May, 1777, General Washington was alarmed to learn that a British captain, a British lieutenant, and two British sergeants were somewhere among his troops, disguised as countrymen. But Washington was never able to find these bold intruders, and no one since has ever been able to find out who they were.

There was another British agent with a "withered" hand, who ought to have been easily identified, and a "middle-sized Indian of about fifty years of age" who carried messages to Sir Henry Clinton in New York. Neither was ever caught, though the patriots knew what they were doing.

At first, American methods of running down spies were rather hit or miss. By the latter half of 1776, however, New York civilian authorities just outside the city had a regular group of counterintelligence agents. These men cooperated successfully with the Continental Army. This spy hunt was largely under the direction of John Jay (who was later to be Chief Justice of the Supreme Court) and Nathaniel Sackett, who a year later would be running a spy ring for General Washington.

The most successful of these spy catchers was the shoemaker Enoch Crosby. He is the only American counterintelligence agent about whom much is known today. This is partly because the American novelist James Fenimore Cooper probably took from him many of the traits of Harvey Birch, the hero of his novel *The Spy*.

Born in Harwich, Massachusetts, Crosby had been brought up in the town of Southeast, near Carmel, New York, and had learned the trade of cordwainer (shoemaker) in Kent, Connecticut, which was then called Phillipstown. He was living in Danbury, Connecticut, when the news of Lexington came.

Crosby was the first man to respond to the call for recruits for a Danbury patriots' company. After serving in the invasion of Canada, he returned to civilian life, as the hardships of the campaign had injured his health. When he was well, in August, 1776, he enlisted again and

started off to join the American forces at Kings-
bridge.

On the way, however, a Westchester Tory
named Bunker mistook Crosby for a fellow Tory.
Seeing his chance, Crosby wormed his way into
the man's confidence so deftly that he was soon
being introduced to more pro-British plotters and
learning all about their schemes. A Tory company, he discovered, was getting ready to join
the British forces within a few days. Crosby was
especially careful to learn the names of all the
officers.

Once he had all this information about the
enemy's plans, Crosby explained to the trusting
Tories that he himself must start for the British
lines at once. Changing direction as soon as he
was out of sight, he made for the house of
"Squire" Young (whose full name is not known),
a member of the American Committee of Safety.
Young took him to John Jay and the Committee
at White Plains, who asked Crosby to help capture the Tory company he had discovered, promising to explain to his regimental commander why
he had not reported for duty. Crosby agreed.

His new boss, John Jay, sent Crosby, posing as
a Tory prisoner, to the ranger company stationed
in White Plains. Crosby soon asked for "an excuse to go out" under guard—the excuse probably
being the lack of indoor sanitary facilities. What-

ever the pretext was, it led him over a fence and into a patch of tall corn, out of sight of the rather green soldier guarding him. Once out of sight, Crosby ran for it. After much banging of muskets, the spy returned to the Tories with a most convincing story of how he had been captured and had escaped.

When the new Tory company was ready to go, Crosby made another stealthy trip to Squire Young's house, four or five miles away. Here he met the American ranger captain from whom he had "escaped." After reporting the Tory company's exact plans, he returned and was arrested with them! To keep up his cover, Crosby was allowed to remain a prisoner for about a week, during which he was moved from one prison to another several times until he could be bailed out.

John Jay now retained Enoch Crosby as a permanent secret agent, still promising to set matters right for him with his regimental commander.

Collecting some tools in a peddler's pack and posing as a wandering shoemaker, Crosby succeeded in getting into another Tory house. It took him only a little while to find out that the Tories were recruiting another company, and he soon managed to scrape an acquaintance with its captain. Invited to enlist, he protested that he did not want to join unless some of his friends were among them. He thus managed to see the muster roll. When Crosby complained there was no one there he knew, the captain let him see other, special, confidential rolls, which he had hidden under a flat stone. The Tory officer then completed his folly by showing the spy a hollow haystack where recruits could be hidden.

By midnight Crosby was back in White Plains, reporting everything to the patriot committee. Before dawn he was again in bed in the house of his Tory host. Next morning he joined the company, though he declined to sign the muster roll until he was within the British lines.

That night, when the whole Tory force met at its captain's house, American mounted rangers closed in. They hauled Crosby himself out of a closet in which he had hidden, and dragged him off in irons with the others, first to White Plains, then to Peekskill, and later to Fort Montgomery (on the Hudson River, near Peekskill). A hint was passed to him that he should keep up his Tory pose till another "escape" could be arranged for him.

At Fort Montgomery, the spy had an embarrassing moment when he met a former teacher who was also a friend of his father's. Horrified "on beholding his favorite pupil, the son of his dearest friend, manacled like a felon, and dragged to prison, with a gang of unprincipled wretches," the teacher passed the bad news on to Enoch Crosby's parents. Since there was nothing else to do, the American spy went right on posing as a Tory, no matter how much it worried his parents. As yet no one suspected what he was really doing, though one American soldier admitted long afterward that he had thought it queer that Crosby, though arrested so many times, always escaped so easily.

Meeting secretly with the Committee again, Crosby was told to sign his future reports "John Smith." Later he used other aliases: Levi Foster, and John or Jacob Brown. When he was returned to prison with orders to manage his own escape, he forced a window during the night and got out. This time he had gone only fifty yards before he encountered a sentry. Again the American patriot had to run for his life, dodging a fusillade of American bullets!

Still posing as a shoemaker, Crosby made his way to Marlboro, New York, on the west bank of the Hudson, near West Point. As "John Smith, a faithful friend to His Majesty," he was introduced to another British officer and was for the third time welcomed as a promising recruit.

In about a week this new Tory company was ready for a rendezvous at Butter Hill, near Cornwall, New York. Again Crosby was ready to report. On November 4, 1776, he sent a trusted courier to the Committee of Safety with a message telling all about the Tories. An answer came back before Crosby set out for the Tory rendezvous in the barn on Butter Hill.

He found the Tory band resting in a haymow so as to be fit for the night's march ahead of them. After a time Crosby heard someone cough outside. Recognizing it as the sign of Colonel William Duer of the Committee of Safety, he coughed in answer. At that, Duer and Captain Townsend, a range officer, with a party of rangers, burst in. Crosby pretended to hide in the hay, since the Tories must not know him for what he was. But when fifty bayonets were plunged into the haymow, he had to come out—fast!

Though Duer knew perfectly well what Crosby was doing, he dared not tell Townsend, who, recognizing this "Tory" prisoner as the same one who had escaped at Fishkill, had him securely tied. In view of Crosby's record of former escapes, he was now jailed in a specially secure room in the house of John Jay, his real employer! Jay was not at home—or did not want to appear. A quick-thinking maid opened some of Jay's best brandy, drugged it, and put both Captain Townsend and his sentry to sleep. She then stole a key from the pocket of the slumbering Townsend and released Crosby.

When he expressed fears for her safety, the girl said slyly, "Dr. Miller's opiates are wonderfully powerful when mixed with brandy."

She then assured him that she herself would "be at Hopewell by the time the alarm is given," and sent him off.

Hampered by his irons, Enoch Crosby paused in a thicket to get rid of them. That he was twice able to free himself of handcuffs would seem incredible if we did not know that other British prisoners had also found American irons insecure and managed to get out of them.

After hiding on West Mountain the rest of the night and all next day, Crosby walked south the following night. Familiar with the countryside, he was able to keep away from farms till he reached a house he knew was a Tory's. Soon afterward, in another farmhouse, he was trapped by two armed patriots. They recognized him as a Tory spy and dragged him off with a warning that "Jay and Duer are determined to make an example of you." Fearing he really might be killed this time, before he could reach either of his two employers, Crosby produced a secret paper, hidden in the lining of his vest, and identified himself.

Hardly had he been released when he was accused by a suspicious Tory, two miles farther on, of being exactly what he was: an American spy.

Crosby bluffed or fought his way to safety and, after making sure Townsend's rangers had left Peekskill, managed to reach Colonel Duer's house. Since he was now under suspicion by both sides, and temporarily useless as a counterintelligence agent, Duer allowed his spy to hide in a German household on Wappinger Creek, in Dutchess County, where another American agent, John Haines, was already reporting Tory activity.

Two days later Crosby was recalled to Fishkill, whence, because that village was now dangerous for him, he was sent on to Hopewell. Here Dr. Miller, the physician who had supplied the opiates used on the guards at John Jay's house, was to find a safe place where Crosby could meet and confer with a member of the Committee that afternoon. Like many medical men of those days, Dr. Miller also ran a drugstore. The doctor was not at home, but Crosby was received by a girl whose face seemed vaguely familiar.

Seeing his puzzled look, she murmured, "Dr. Miller's opiates, you recollect, are very powerful when mixed with brandy."

She was the maid at Jay's house, whom Crosby had seen only in the dark. This resourceful girl gave "Mr. Brown" (the name Crosby was using at this time) a seat by the fire, to await the doctor's return. He spent the evening listening to a lively discussion by the doctor's waiting patients of his own exploits as a British spy! He found it interesting to hear the local gossip about himself, and to learn he had such a bad reputation.

Presently John Jay himself came in, ostensibly to buy medicine. While Crosby politely held his stirrup, Jay whispered an order to return to the German farmer, to avoid discovery. Crosby obediently did so and remained on the farm as the peaceful cobbler "Jacob Brown," making shoes for the family until well on in December, 1776. He was then ordered to travel, by a roundabout way, through Bennington, Vermont, to Sharon, Connecticut, and report on Tories there.

To make his pose as a loyal subject of King George III more convincing, the Committee supplied him with a bundle of genuine British proclamations. These offered pardon to rebels. General William Howe had caused them to be spread about the countryside. Though this made it easy to approach Tories, it might have cost Crosby his life if Americans had found him carrying papers of this sort.

Returning to Fishkill, he was then sent off to Pawling, New York, in the general direction of Wappinger Creek. The patriot spy John Haines had reported on December 23, 1776, that a Tory militia company would soon rendezvous at the

home of a certain Captain Chapman. A few days
later another patriot agent, named Nicholas
Brower, warned Nathaniel Sackett that there
would be a Tory rendezvous—probably the same
one—between Fishkill and Wappinger Creek.

As soon as Haines's report came in, on December 23, the Committee decided to have their dependable spy catcher, Enoch Crosby, "use his
utmost Art to discover the designs, Places of Resort, and route of certain disaffected Persons . . .
who have form'd a Design of Joining the Enemy."
He was given all the information the Committee
had: a double set of passes—one American, the
other British, enabling him to pass both lines—
also thirty dollars, a horse, new clothing, and a
new name. This time he was "Levi Foster."
Nathaniel Sackett, instead of Jay, took charge of
his mission.

A week later, on December 30, John Jay told
Sackett to alert Captain Peter Van Gaasbeek's
militia company to apprehend "certain persons."
In five days Sackett had preliminary reports from
both his spies, "Foster" (Crosby) and Haines. Six
days later, on January 10, he suddenly remembered that something must be done to protect
Crosby, and he wrote Captain Van Gaasbeek:

> I had almost forgot to give you directions
> to give our friend an opportunity of making
> his escape. Upon our plan you will take him

prisoner with this party you are now waiting for. His name is Enoch Crosby alias John Brown. I could wish that he may escape before you bring him two miles on your way to Committee. . . . By no means neglect this friend of ours.

Meantime Crosby had once again joined a Tory company of recruits and had also made the acquaintance of a Tory physician, Dr. Prosser, who at the moment had as a patient the lieutenant of the Tory company. The unsuspecting doctor rashly told Crosby all about the Tory plans, their leaders, and their houses, and gave him a chance to make the Tory lieutenant's acquaintance! The physician never suspected that Crosby was not a real Tory. After all, Crosby was in the Tory company. He was acting like a good king's man. He inspired confidence in everybody. It shows that Crosby was clever and audacious—a good spy.

On February 9, 1777, Dr. Prosser brought Crosby a message from Silvester Handy, a Tory agent; all was ready for the recruits to assemble. Crosby was to go to the house of Enoch Hoag, another Tory. Here he stayed four or five days, taking notes of his host's disloyal talk, picking up information, identifying the men who were guiding Tories to New York City, and learning all about a force under Captain Zebulon Ross,

Jr., which included Connecticut Tory recruits. He went from one Tory house to another, identifying more and more British agents, and, on the night appointed, was back at Hoag's to join the Tory recruits assembled there.

Seeing there was no time to notify the American committee (which was holding Van Gaasbeek's company in readiness for a raid), Crosby passed the word of the Tory forces being assembled to a patriot, Colonel Andrew Morehouse, who lived only three miles from Hoag. Grimly, Morehouse promised "they should be attended to."

Some of the Tories arriving at Hoag's said they had noticed "a gathering under arms at old Morehouse's," but before anything could be done about it the Americans were on them, with shouts of "Stand, stand!" Hoag's house was surrounded. Tories who tried to run away were met by American militia, no matter which way they turned. The whole band was caught and lashed together in pairs.

Crosby tried to beg off, explaining that he was too lame to walk. Morehouse, who knew perfectly well who Crosby was and what he was doing, had to appear stern in front of the other captives.

"You shall go dead or alive," said he to Crosby. "If in no other way, you shall be carried on the horse with me."

On reaching Morehouse's home, Crosby was released, and Colonel Morehouse marched his other prisoners off to the Committee, reporting that he had acted on information from "the Immissary." Of course, the Committee knew that the Immissary was their dependable spy, Enoch Crosby.

But in spite of all efforts to conceal his identity and make things look natural, Crosby's series of successes had by now destroyed his usefulness as a secret agent. He had joined one Tory company after another; each company he had joined had been seized, but he himself had always escaped. There had been too many such coincidences. And since he was a marked man among Westchester Tories, the patriots decided to send him to Albany, where he was unknown. As smallpox had broken out there, he was sent first to his friend Dr. Miller for inoculation. Crosby spent some time at Albany, acting openly in the transfer of Tory property.

When John Jay turned to other duties, and Nathaniel Sackett went to manage, from New Jersey, an espionage ring working on Manhattan Island, where Crosby had no contacts, the spy was finally allowed to withdraw from the secret service entirely.

At last his parents were allowed to know the truth about their son. He returned to live with a brother in the Highlands, until Tory attempts to get revenge became too dangerous. Once a bullet fired through a window just grazed Crosby's neck! A few nights after this attempt to kill him, armed Tories burst into the house. There were shots, and then the leader yelled, "Let us pound him to death!" By the time they got through, Crosby lay unconscious, and the gang probably thought him dead.

It took several months for Crosby to recover from this assault. He then went back to the army and served in the New York Continental Line until the end of the war. But compared with his adventures as a secret agent, when he was living a never-ending dangerous game of super hide-and-seek, he must have found even active duty at the front a little dull.

III. Spies in New York, New Jersey,
and Pennsylvania, 1766-1777

The Newest Secret Service

SWIFTLY, HOPELESSLY, General Washington was
driven out of New York City, then out of New
York State, then across New Jersey, and finally
into Philadelphia. When at last he had the rem-
nants of his dwindling army safely over the Delaware River, the general finally began to do
something he should have done much earlier: he
set up intelligence nets. He established one net
in New Jersey, where he expected to attack the
enemy in a few weeks. He set up another around
Philadelphia, where he feared the enemy might
soon attack him.

For these espionage systems, he had to have
new American spies who were familiar enough
with the local people to know who was Whig

and who was Tory, and who understood local geography, customs, and habits. These new secret agents were to supply the Continental Army with constant and accurate military intelligence, no matter where the army went, no matter what the enemy was doing. General Washington set up his new intelligence system in New Jersey, where his army's immediate need was greatest; then inside and around New York City, the British base; and then around Philadelphia, where there was certain to be fighting sooner or later.

Within a very short time American espionage in New York City was much increased. By November, 1776, General Mercer, who had failed to get an agent to Staten Island in July, was able to send a skilled observer into New York City. To this day no one knows who he was, but he came back with a full report of British intentions, troop movements, losses, and reinforcements. When the Americans were forced back beyond New Brunswick, New Jersey, in the first day or two of December, another daring secret agent quietly dropped off, in preparation for eighteen months of undetected espionage.

Still other new spies were soon at work. A screen of additional secret agents spread out into New Jersey, far beyond the American front. Joshua and John Mersereau, two of the men who helped to direct this operation, always believed they saved Washington's army from total destruction. They may have been right. Too weak to face the British forces, Washington, after retreating into Pennsylvania, had tried to seize all the boats on the Delaware. If he could lay hands on all of them, the British could not cross to attack him.

Some of the local Tories, seeing what Washington was doing, had sunk boats in the river, thus concealing them. They meant to raise them from the water when General Howe's men arrived and needed ferries. But Joshua Mersereau ran a ferry himself and owned a boat yard which built small craft. He knew all about such tricks. The two brothers found the boats where the Tories had hidden them and took them all away. The redcoats could not cross. Thanks to these two men, General Washington had a chance to rest and reorganize his army. Later he was able to cross the Delaware himself and defeat the redcoats at Trenton.

One spy—and probably more—had been dropped off some time before the Continental Army reached Pennsylvania. General Washington soon had other agents wandering through the Jersey camps of British Generals Leslie and Howard, and of the British allies—the German Colonels von Donop and Rall. Patriot horsemen, dressed like ordinary countryfolk, rode through

New Jersey as they pleased, "talking Tory" loudly and collecting military intelligence quietly. Some of them peddled tobacco. It was an easy way to get into the enemy camp, since the Hessians and other Germans were always eager for a smoke. These intelligence missions were so perfectly concealed that the identities of most of these spies are unknown even to this day.

The first clear demonstration of how much the American intelligence service had improved was the capture of Trenton, the day after Christmas, 1776. Twelve days before he crossed the river, General Washington ordered his generals to look for "some Person who can be engaged to cross the River as a spy." Washington was afraid the British still meant to cross the Delaware themselves, and he wanted to find out whether they were building boats, collecting horses, or bringing up more troops.

Boats, especially, were a clue to the enemy's intentions. All through the Revolution, intelligence officers on both sides spent a good deal of time trying to find out whether the other army was assembling small boats. If they *were*, it meant they planned to cross a river or some other body of water. The spies had only to look for the nearest water, and they could guess pretty accurately where the enemy was going to attack.

British spies outside New York City always

watched this matter carefully. They knew the Americans could not attack Long Island or Manhattan Island (New York City) unless General Washington had boats enough to carry hundreds of soldiers across at the same time. General Washington had the same idea about the British.

Before he made his celebrated attack at Trenton, he wanted to "get some person into the town itself." This spy was to see what Colonel Rall and the Hessians were doing there. Unfortunately, Trenton was an especially dangerous place for American spies. It was full of Tories who were quick to recognize them and eager to betray them. Some secret agents flatly refused to enter Trenton at all. On December 10, however, Washington was able to send in one man. As usual, the general wanted to know whether the enemy was building boats. When the spy brought back word that they were not, the general could be sure the enemy did not intend to cross the Delaware and attack him.

Still, if he himself meant to cross the Delaware and attack the British, he would have to have a good deal more information than that. No matter what the danger, another secret agent would have to go into Trenton and get it. Before long, General Washington found the right man.

The courageous weaver and butcher, John Honeyman, of Griggstown, New Jersey, accepted the ignominious position of pretending to be a Tory and a disloyal American. About the middle of December he fled from his home; and Washington, as had been arranged, immediately denounced him as a traitor.

Denunciations like this became a favorite trick of the general's. He knew British spies were lurking about his camp, even though he couldn't find them. These enemy spies were sure to find out that Washington had denounced a man. That would ensure the American spy a warm welcome when he "fled" to the British.

Perhaps General Washington overdid his denunciation of John Honeyman just a little bit. Quite unintentionally he stirred up a mob of patriots. Led by a hotheaded eighteen-year-old, they raided the Honeyman home at Griggstown, looking for the supposed Tory. After they had searched the house in vain, Mrs. Honeyman had to do something. To get rid of them, she brought out a paper signed by Washington himself:

It is hereby ordered that the wife and children of John Honeyman, of Griggstown, the notorious Tory, now within the British lines, and probably acting the part of a spy, shall be and hereby are protected from all harm and annoyance from any quarter until further orders.

The commander in chief didn't say *which side* Honeyman was spying for! He did add one more line:

This furnishes no protection for Honeyman himself.

Since it takes a soldier's eye to observe a military installation, John Honeyman was an ideal man for his mission. He had served in the French and Indian War. He had been in General Wolfe's bodyguard at Quebec, had seen Wolfe fall. He had been one of the men who carried the general off the field, "walking most of the way in blood," as he described it later. As a British veteran with a fine record, his interest in the Trenton garrison would, therefore, seem natural and he would be above suspicion.

The spy and General Washington had been casual acquaintances for some time. Probably they first met in Philadelphia about the time Washington was attending the Continental Congress. They met again as the Continental Army was beginning its retreat across New Jersey. Washington must have asked Honeyman to spy for him about this time.

When Honeyman agreed, he was told to leave his family and go over to the British, posing as a butcher and horse trader. In such a role it would seem natural for him to be continually wandering about the countryside from farm to farm. Supposedly he would be looking for cattle to slaughter and horses to trade. The Hessians in Trenton would be buying beef. Officers were always glad to talk with a horse trader.

When the time was ripe, Honeyman was to venture a little too far into the country in search of cattle. He would go far enough to make sure the Americans captured him. Once he was a prisoner, he could leave the rest to General Washington. Thus, for some time, the spy was able to study the enemy camps at both New Brunswick and Trenton. He noted the lax discipline and inadequate defenses at Trenton. It was easy enough for the experienced soldier to learn about Hessian troop dispositions, artillery positions, and outguards. As late as December 22, 1776, Honeyman was still going about with the enemy in their pursuit of wandering detachments of American troops. Apparently he knew about Washington's plans for an attack on Trenton. He set off toward the Delaware River to report at exactly the right time.

Orders went out from American headquarters that Honeyman must be arrested on sight. Only —and on this point orders were very definite— this dangerous rascal was to be brought in *alive*. The commander in chief wanted to question him personally. (That was true, too. Of course General Washington wanted to question him personally, though not for the reasons implied!)

Presently, as he wandered along through the cold, raw New Jersey countryside, looking for a chance to be captured, Honeyman saw two American scouts trying to hide behind some bushes. To keep up his pose as a butcher, Honeyman went into the next field. He picked out one from a herd of cows and drove her, with a great cracking of his whip and a good deal of shouting, toward the bushes. When the scouts emerged to catch him, the "Tory" Honeyman looked guilty, left his cow, and started running. He managed to slip on a handy patch of ice, was caught, fought to get free, and yielded only when pistols pointed at his head. It all seemed very natural, as it was meant to seem.

The scouts marched their prisoner in triumph to their general. Washington looked serious. He ordered the room cleared. He alone would interview this sinister "turncoat." The general and the spy were alone for half an hour. Then, about sunset, the prisoner was put into a log hut, to await court-martial in the morning.

A fire broke out nearby, almost at once. (Queer, wasn't it, that there should be a fire the moment Honeyman was locked up?) The sentries guarding the hut quit their posts—which sentries are not supposed to do—to help put out the fire. When they got back their prisoner was gone. No one understood how he got away!

Within a few hours the clever Honeyman, still carrying out orders for his crafty general, was telling the enemy commander in Trenton all about his adventures. Having been in the American camp, he could assure the Hessian Colonel Rall that he need have no fear of an American attack for a long time to come. Colonel Rall and his Hessians could forget about it and have a good time celebrating Christmas! And that is exactly what they did.

Having planted this false information on behalf of General Washington, Honeyman set off for New Brunswick. He had to get out of the way. He well knew that American troops would soon be falling in for their attack on Trenton. They might already be on the march. John Honeyman didn't want to be anywhere around Colonel Rall when the Americans hit Trenton.

Everyone knows about that silent crossing of the Delaware River on the cold morning after Christmas Day, 1776—how General Washington assailed the unprepared Hessians while they were sleeping off their Christmas celebration, and won a famous victory. What has not been known is the part played by the American secret intelligence service, whose work is never publicized and usually not even admitted.

When the move toward Trenton began, General Washington took further precautions. Three volunteers in farmers' clothing—which made them technically spies—preceded the American column, like the antennae, or "feelers," of an insect. These men knew the country perfectly. Two came from Hopewell, New Jersey. One lived in Trenton itself. They were to reconnoiter Hessian outposts and prevent Tories from carrying warning. But there were not enough of them. General Washington had wanted twelve such men, but could not find them. As a result, in spite of all precautions, one Tory did reach town with warning of the raid. But Colonel Rall, deep in his Christmas festivities, would not talk to the man. Nor did he read the note this devoted subject of the king insisted on sending in by a servant. The paper with its unread warning was still in Colonel Rall's pocket as he lay dying after the American attack.

The Americans had hardly returned from their victory at Trenton when the new intelligence service again proved its value. A little while earlier, Washington had written to Colonel John Cadwalader to "spare no pains or expense to get Intelligence of the Enemy's motions."

Colonel Cadwalader went diligently to work. Within a few days after Trenton he sent the commander in chief a sketch map. On this, from spies' reports, he had been able to plot all the approaches to Princeton—defenses, artillery locations, and the exact spots where the redcoats were quartered. When General Washington slipped away from the startled Cornwallis and bore down on Princeton a few days later, he knew exactly what he would find there, thanks to the spies. The result was another great victory.

American espionage achieved one of its most impudently daring and successful exploits in New Jersey and New York about this time. The hero was Lieutenant Lewis J. Costigin, who, before he joined the army, had been a merchant in New Brunswick, New Jersey. The lieutenant was first sent out as a spy a few days after the victory at Trenton. General Washington had suddenly found that Cornwallis was marching through New Jersey against him. He wanted to know what forces the British had in New Brunswick.

Colonel Matthias Ogden, commanding the First New Jersey, was told to find a suitable person to go into New Brunswick in disguise and find out the strength of the British forces then in town. This spy was to make a special effort to study their baggage train. Its size might be a clue to enemy strength and intentions. Colonel Ogden asked Costigin to volunteer, because Costigin came from New Brunswick, and his family was still living there.

Instructed by George Washington in person, the lieutenant went straight into the town to procure all the information he possibly could. While Costigan was on his way back, January 1, 1777, British cavalry captured him. Whether he entered New Brunswick in disguise or not, no one knows now. He was certainly in uniform again when the British caught him, and, not being in disguise, he was treated not as a spy, but as an ordinary prisoner of war. He was sent back to New York City, where he was freed on a parole that lasted for nearly two years.

Parole released an officer from confinement and allowed him to move about freely, within limits. He had to give his word of honor—that is, parole—not to try to escape.

By the following August, First Lieutenant Costigin had done something important enough to make no less a person than General Washington himself want to have him exchanged. Orders went out on August 21 to get the lieutenant back by the speediest means. At the same time General Washington warned the American officers who were managing the exchange of prisoners not to seem overanxious to get Costigin back. That might make the British suspicious. Then they would want to keep him. Immediately on release, the lieutenant was to be sent straight to headquarters to report to General Washington himself.

Such interest on the part of the commander in chief in a mere junior officer meant Costigin had done something so important that he had attracted the attention of the "high brass." From New York City, Costigin had managed to get into secret communication with American intelligence. He still had the secret information he had gained in New Brunswick, just before his capture. Perhaps he had sent some in.

Three weeks later, on September 18, 1778, Costigin was formally exchanged. This freed him from the obligations of parole. Yet in spite of that he did not return to his own army, as an exchanged prisoner is supposed to do. Instead, acting on orders from General Stirling and Colonel Ogden (who had selected Costigin for his original espionage mission), the lieutenant simply stayed in New York. Perhaps he pretended to have Tory leanings and to be unwilling to rejoin his own army. Perhaps British officers in New York were so used to seeing him around as a paroled prisoner that it never occurred to them that Lieutenant Costigin ought to be back with his own army. It was an ideal situation if he wanted to spy on the British, because technically he was not a spy at all. He was in uniform. Everyone knew he was an American officer.

Protected by this amazing cover, Costigin went to work sending in reports under the signature of "Z." With a soldier's trained eye, Lieutenant Costigin was able to find out all about the personal movements of Sir Henry Clinton and other British officers and leading Tory figures, as well as about British troop movements, shipping, bread shortage, and supply of British rations. He could get all this valuable information by walking through Manhattan streets, and chatting with British officers who had come to know him and grown used to seeing him around during his long captivity.

The amusing aspect of this paradoxical situation is that the enemy could not legally have hanged him, even if they had found out what he was doing. He was in New York perfectly openly. He was in uniform. He was no longer on parole.

However, Costigin did not push his luck too far. He stayed as long as he thought it was safe. Then, on January 17, 1779, four months after his exchange, he rejoined the army he belonged to.

It is clear that nobody ever told the scrupulous Washington just how sharp a game his intelligence men were playing. When Costigin failed to report to him three weeks after he had been formally exchanged upon Washington's order, the general still did not know what had really happened. In fact he was puzzled. There had been some mistake, he thought, in executing his orders.

Nobody had told General Washington, either, that Lieutenant Costigin was, in reality, that fine spy, "Z." The "Z" reports were sent on by Colonel Ogden, through General Stirling, to Washington. The commander in chief thought them very valuable. Probably Ogden and Stirling never did tell their general who "Z" really was. On March 15, 1779, two months after Costigin's return to the Continental Army, Washington was asking what had become of "Z." He wondered whether a new spy was needed to replace him!

Poor Costigin, meantime, had spent, in gathering intelligence, £113 of his own money. Washington at last learned the truth—three years later—when he received Lieutenant Costigin's petition for payment of his expenses!

Meanwhile the British had been pushed back in New Jersey and the American army was settled in Morristown. After the Battle of Princeton, a whole new set of intelligence snares was laid for the redcoats. The network included not only New Jersey, but also New York and Pennsylvania. The extent of the secret-service activity that went on then is shown by the money spent on it, as recorded in General Washington's accounts. Lieutenant Colonel Joseph Reed received $238 in January 1777; the Westchester spy catcher, Nathaniel Sackett, got $500 to do some spying of his own in February; Major General Adam Stephen, $200 in April; Major General Benjamin Lincoln, $450 in May.

General Heath, ordered to send spies to New York in mid-January, 1777, had a regular network established there by April.

Espionage in New Jersey was in several hands, but it was kept under such secrecy that it is impossible to find out today what some of the American spies were doing. All anyone can find out now is that the spies were there. General Israel Putnam was told on January 5, 1777, to have some spies, dressed like farmers, watching for a British advance from New York City. "Old Put" undoubtedly carried out his orders, but that is all anybody knows. Another of Washington's intelligence officers at this time was Colonel Elias Boudinot, who combined military intelligence with the care of British prisoners.

About the same time, Washington got in touch with Nathaniel Sackett. He was the man who, with Colonel William Duer, had been active in counterintelligence in Westchester County, New York. He had employed Enoch Crosby.

Sackett had made a good beginning in Westchester County in 1776. In February, 1777, General Washington called him to headquarters, gave him money for expenses, and told him to find spies who would mingle with the British forces. Sackett knew just where to find the right people. Within a few weeks his spy network was at work, and one of his secret agents had started for New York.

Sackett soon found two more volunteers willing to go inside the enemy's lines and live there. One went to New Brunswick, the other to Perth Amboy.

Whoever they were, these men were well qualified for their work. One had a son who was a colonel in the British forces; he was able to get letters of introduction to two other British officers. That meant the British would think he was a Tory sympathizer—just what the Americans wanted them to think. To make his cover story still more plausible, this man was authorized to take eight or ten actual deserters over to the British side. The Americans were willing enough to let these men go over to the enemy, if it would really help them cover a spy. The skill with which this particular spy was eased into British territory shows how much American intelligence had learned in the few months since brave Nathan Hale was sent, unprepared, to an heroic but useless death.

By the end of March, 1777, Sackett had a still better agent—the loyal wife of a disloyal American. Her husband had already gone over to the enemy. For his disloyalty, the wife had personally suffered at the hands of the patriots, who had taken some of her grain supplies. She herself remained a loyal American in spite of this treatment, but it would give her something believable to complain about when she reached General Howe—something that would make her "Toryism" seem genuine. If suspicious British intelligence officers investigated her story, they would find it was perfectly true.

She joined the British about the end of March, and within a few days had important information for Nathaniel Sackett. She reported that the British were building boats to use in an attack on Philadelphia.

It was the spring of 1777. General Washington had already strongly suspected that the British would eventually try to seize Philadelphia, when Nathaniel Sackett's unknown woman spy reported that this was General Howe's intention. Then an unlucky British spy—caught and hanged in the city—provided confirmation. He had been trying to secure Delaware River pilots. It was discovered that other British spies were examining the river and sounding its depths. Such information could be useful only in attacking Philadelphia.

When Howe did finally start from New York, July 23, 1777, an American spy aboard a British man-o'-war in New York Harbor watched his ships sail. A report went to General Washington the very next day. Though he still did not know exactly where the British fleet would land its cargo of redcoats, General Washington acted swiftly. He couldn't protect Philadelphia permanently, but when the British marched in, a first-class American spy system was waiting to report everything they did.

After that, strange to say, Sackett's efficient spy system vanished from the records. Probably it was absorbed by another new and efficient American spy network which was coming into existence about this time. This was established by the Mersereau brothers, Joshua and John, who had already saved the army by discovering the boats the Tories had hidden in the Delaware.

One of the greatest of George Washington's many great qualities was the way he could learn from his own mistakes. He had indeed failed to establish an efficient espionage network on Staten Island, Long Island, and Manhattan; and his mistake had cost the Americans dearly. But now, even with the tremendous responsibilities of getting his beaten army to safety, he made extensive arrangements for intelligence.

Even as the British had regained the upper hand and were driving him relentlessly back through New Jersey, Washington asked Joshua Mersereau to help get the secret information he was going to need. Mersereau suggested his son, the younger John Mersereau. Though he was a brave and patriotic young man, eager to serve his country, John Mersereau could not join the army. One of his arms was so badly crippled that he could not hold a musket. But he was perfectly willing to take risks, and the crippled arm was no handicap in the military intelligence service.

Young Mersereau agreed to remain in New Brunswick after the American forces were gone. He would let the British find him there, apparently a harmless civilian. Then he would work his way to Staten Island. The result was eighteen months of highly successful espionage by young Mersereau himself, and the later development of a large intelligence network by his father, brother, uncle, and numerous intrepid assistants.

At first John Mersereau himself remained constantly within the British lines on Staten Island. As courier he used another young man, John Parker, who had worked in his father's shipyard. After a few secret trips into American-held territory, Parker was caught and thrown into a British prison, where he soon died.

After this, young John Mersereau, forced to assume the risks of a courier as well as a spy, began to slip away from Staten Island on a raft, carrying his secret papers in a bottle tied to a string. It seems evident that he towed the weighted bottle in the river. If challenged, he could let go the string. The bottle with the secret papers would sink.

At Shooter's Island, between Staten Island and New Jersey, young Mersereau put his papers under a large stone. Sometimes he picked up instructions that had been left there for him. Light signals told when papers had been hidden.

Once, hearing that his father was in Elizabeth, New Jersey, young Mersereau boldly joined him there—a piece of rashness that was nearly his undoing. Finding an old skiff on the grass in an unguarded part of Staten Island, he used it, instead of his raft, to cross to New Jersey, and went on to Elizabeth. Dawn was breaking before he was ready to start back. He had to lie concealed all day in an old barn before setting out for Staten Island the next night.

Meantime, however, someone had noticed the disappearance of the skiff, and a sentry was watching the spot. When the spy heard his challenge, he crept on his hands and feet to a ditch along which he could run without being exposed to the sentry's fire. When a bullet whacked into a post just over his head, Mersereau jumped out of the ditch and ran for his lodgings. Pursued by several men, he reached the house and shut himself in his room. His pursuers, bursting in after him, were met by a crusty and very drunk British major who also lodged there. He threw them out, swearing "there were no rebels in the house where he lodged." In the darkness no one had recognized Mersereau.

After a few such escapes, Mersereau eventually came under British suspicion. Realizing this, he slipped away, joined the Americans, and assisted in caring for the prisoners captured from Burgoyne's army.

His sixteen-year-old brother replaced him, going back and forth to Staten Island in a small skiff (normally kept hidden in the cellar of a relative's house). Papers were collected for him by still another Mersereau, Paul. He had managed to remain, unsuspected, on Staten Island.

At about this time, Colonel Elias Dayton, a New Jersey officer who became active in military intelligence, began to build up another group of secret agents. By July 5, 1777, General Washington was able to tell Congress, "I keep people constantly on Staten Island, who give me daily information of the operations of the enemy."

The network grew so rapidly that on July 26 Washington told the colonel to send twenty spies to Staten Island to observe the enemy's troops, positions, guards, and strength.

The American commander in chief had now, after this first year of the war, mastered the intricacies of military intelligence. He wanted no more untrained amateurs—like poor Nathan Hale—to die uselessly. He told Major General Thomas Mifflin, "Give the persons you pitch upon, proper lessons."

At least once, however, the American intelligence officers "pitched upon" the wrong man, as they soon discovered. They made the mistake of trying to use schoolmaster Thomas Long, inelegantly known in Rahway, New Jersey, as "Bunk Eye" because of his too prominent eyes. He was sent to Philadelphia in April, 1777, as an American spy. Two days later it turned out that the man had Tory sympathies. He might already be spying for the British. General Washington had to send hasty orders for his arrest, and he was eventually hanged.

Codes, Masks, and Ciphers

No MATTER HOW HARD American counterintelligence worked, it could not catch all the Tory spies immediately. Some of them were never caught. Some were not even suspected for the next hundred years or more. Even now, in our own times, a few have probably never been detected. Samuel Wallis, one of the worst, was not unmasked until a few years ago, though he was deeply implicated in Benedict Arnold's treason. Neither, for that matter, were several loyal American spies ever suspected by the British. In fact it is very probable that a great many spies on both sides were never detected during the Revolution and will never be discovered now.

As Burgoyne's mixed force of British, Germans, and Indians moved southward from Canada in the summer of 1777, more and more secret couriers began to pass up and down the Hudson Valley between Burgoyne's field headquarters and General Sir Henry Clinton's headquarters in New York City. They came and went in an almost continuous stream. After Burgoyne had started south, the only way for the two generals to keep in touch with each other was through these couriers, who had to travel straight through American-held territory. Since they were disguised as ordinary civilians and were out of uniform, these messengers were technically spies, and could be hanged as such if caught. Sometimes, instead of making the whole dangerous journey, they met midway and exchanged messages. Livingston's Manor, between Rhinebeck and Kinderhook, New York, was one rendezvous for such Tory couriers.

It was so dangerous and difficult for these couriers to get through that one of them lost his courage and did not even try. This was Henry Williams, of Peekskill, who had been paid to carry a letter to Burgoyne in July, 1777. Instead, he simply stopped on the way and turned his letter over to the patriots, thereby making sure he would not be hanged. Another, Francis Hogel, and his guide, William Showers, were caught the same month. Hogel admitted that several of Burgoyne's messengers had never returned. (Perhaps because they too became so frightened they simply gave up their missions.)

The British took every precaution to conceal the messages their secret couriers carried. Sometimes the message was written on long, narrow strips of paper and then stuck inside the hollow quills of large feathers. A number of these long strips of paper which unknown spies once carried, at the risk of their lives, to Sir Henry Clinton, are still to be seen among his headquarters papers. A better way of preserving secrecy was the use of code "masks." These were sheets of paper with openings cut into them. The real message was written in these openings, after which the lines were filled in to make the whole thing read as if it were something altogether different. The officer receiving the letter had only to lay his mask over the page to have the original message appear. Several of these masks also remain among Clinton's papers.

One such letter from Sir Henry Clinton to Burgoyne, August 10, 1777, reads like an ordinary message until it is covered with a paper mask, which has a large opening in the shape of a dumbbell cut out of it. Laid upon Sir Henry's apparently harmless communication, the mask at once reveals the secret.

Without the mask, the whole letter reads:

You will have heard, Dr Sir I doubt not long before this can have reached you that Sir W. Howe is gone from hence. The Rebels imagine that he is gone to the Southward. By this time however he has filled Cheasapeak bay with surprize and terror.

Washington marched the greatest part of the Rebels to Philadelphia in order to oppose Sir W^{ms} army. I hear he is now returned upon finding none of our troops landed but am not sure of this. great part of his troops are returned for certain. I am sure this [illegible] must be vain to them. I am left to command here, half my force may I am sure defend every thing here with as much safety I shall therefore send Sir W. 4 or 5 bat^n I have too small a force to invade the New England provinces, they are too weak to make any effectual efforts against me and you do not want any diversion in your favour I can therefore very well spare him 1500 men I shall try something certainly towards the close of the year not till then at any rate. It may be of use to inform you that report says all yields to you. I own to you that the business will quickly be over now. Sr W.'s move just at the time has been Capital Washingtons have been the worst he could take in every respect I sincerely give you much

joy on your success and am with great
sincerity. . . .

Seen through the mask, the meaning is altogether different. The letter now reads:

Sir
W. Howe
is gone to the
Cheasapeak bay with
the greatest part of the
army. I hear he is now
landed but am not
certain. I am
left to command
here with
too small a force
to make any effectual
diversion in your favour
I shall try something cer
at any rate. It may be of use
to you. I own to you I think
Sʳ W.'s move just at this time
the worst he could take
much joy on your succ

Sir Henry Clinton was clever enough to in-
clude a little military information (mostly false)
in the part of the letter that the enemy would
understand, in case it was captured.

Different shapes could be used for the masks.
Clinton, in addition to his dumbbell mask, also

used a mask with oblong holes to reveal the concealed message.

One of the most tragic of these secret British messengers was the spy with the silver bullet. By the fall of 1777, American General Gates had a whole American army closely pressing Burgoyne and cutting him off from Sir Henry Clinton. But a British victory would still be certain if Clinton could bring up the Hudson an army strong enough so that he and Burgoyne could crush Gates between them. Clinton, however, was having trouble in getting enough troops, as General Howe had taken most of the redcoats from New York to Philadelphia, where he faced General Washington.

It was very important that Burgoyne should get word that Clinton was doing his best to advance from New York City up the Hudson to help him. Burgoyne's plans depended on Clinton's support.

There was in Burgoyne's army a captain named Campbell, who had succeeded in secretly making his way around (or through) Gates's army with a message asking Clinton whether Burgoyne ought to advance or retreat. It had taken Captain Campbell nearly a week to make this short trip. The reply had to be delivered faster.

Sir Henry, who had already started to meet Burgoyne, replied in a dispatch from American

Fort Montgomery, a little way up the Hudson, which he had just captured. His letter was written on thin silk, instead of paper, and it said:

> *Nous y voilà* [here we are] and nothing now between us but Gates. I sincerely hope this little success of ours may facilitate your operations. In answer to your letter of the 28th Sepr. by C.C. [Captain Campbell]—I shall only say, I cannot presume to order or even advice [advise] for reasons obvious. I heartily wish you success, & that &c.

After his small bit of silk had been rolled up and concealed in an oval silver ball about the size of a rifle bullet, it was handed to Daniel Taylor, a young man who had been promised promotion if he got through alive. The bullet was made of silver, so that the spy could swallow it, if necessary, without injury from corrosion in his stomach. Out of pure good nature, Taylor also took some other letters, which were more dangerous. Various British officers had asked him to take personal letters of their own.

Taylor concealed the bullet in his hair (which was easy to do in those days when gentlemen wore long hair, plaited in queues) and set out. This was not the first time he had made this dangerous journey.

One day ahead of Taylor, Captain Campbell also started back to Burgoyne, carrying the same

message. The two had been careful to keep
apart, for two secret couriers on the same errand
dared not go together. They had to keep apart
so that if one were caught, the other would still
have a chance to get through. Probably Captain
Campbell reached Burgoyne safely, after the
surrender or just before. Certainly the Americans never caught him. But his message, if it
ever did reach Burgoyne, came too late to do
the British general any good.

Taylor had no way of knowing that, from
the start, he had been in even greater danger
than a spy usually faces. There was very little
hope he would get through alive, for the Americans were already on the lookout for him. Henry
Williams of Peekskill, the British courier who
in July had lost his Tory courage and given up
the spy's dangerous game of hide-and-seek, had
already told the Americans all he knew about
other British agents. Williams had especially
warned that there was "a person who constantly
plyes between York & Canada his Name Taylor,
his dress a blue Camblet Coat with white facings
and silver Epaulets." After that, every spy catcher
in the Hudson Valley was keeping an eye open
for poor Taylor.

Unaware of his unusual danger, he had gone
only a few miles when he ran into American
troops at New Windsor, not far downstream from

West Point. By that time Taylor had, as companion, a man named Isaac Vanvleek, though nobody knows who he was or where he came from.

After losing their way, the pair fell in with an outpost or patrol from Webb's Connecticut Regiment. The soldiers happened to be wearing scarlet uniforms, taken from a captured British transport. The American troops were so hard up for clothing that they wore anything, even enemy uniforms, if they were lucky enough to capture any. Worst of all for Taylor, Webb's Regiment had been Nathan Hale's original regiment. The British had hanged Hale. Webb's Regiment was not in the humor to deal gently with enemy spies.

When Taylor saw the red coats of his own army, he assumed he was in friendly hands. He said some things which his captors thought suspicious. A quick-witted sergeant, guessing what Taylor really was, agreed to take him to "General Clinton," as the prisoner demanded. It was easy to deceive the luckless spy. So far, he had gone only a little way beyond his own lines. He knew that General *Sir Henry* Clinton was at Fort Montgomery, ten miles down the river. Hence he was not alarmed, and did not try to get rid of his silver bullet and his incriminating letters.

Imagine his feelings when he was led before the American, General *George* Clinton, in New Windsor, and saw a strange officer in American uniform!

The wretched spy suddenly realized his peril and knew it was too late. Overcome with terror, he cried out, "I am lost!" and swallowed his silver bullet.

Everybody around saw him swallow it. Everybody knew it must contain something important. Dr. Moses Higby, who had an office near headquarters, supplied "a very strong emetic." Taylor, held down and forced to swallow it, vomited the bullet. Instantly he snatched it up, swallowed it again, and tried to escape. By this time he had lost his head completely. Escape was impossible. He was seized at once.

Only when General Clinton threatened to hang him and cut the bullet out of his stomach did the miserable Taylor submit to a second dose. The American authorities got what they were after and, upon unscrewing the two halves of the silver bullet, found Sir Henry's message to Burgoyne.

Taylor was court-martialed and sentenced to death on October 14, 1777. His execution was ordered two days later. But Vanvleek may have told enough to save his own life. Nobody knows what ever did happen to Vanvleek. In any event, as the Americans moved on up the Hudson, they met a horseman who came galloping down with the wonderful news that Burgoyne had surrendered to General Gates. The Americans had won the day.

In part at least—perhaps entirely—Burgoyne's surrender at Saratoga was due to Alexander Bryan, a daring American secret agent whose name is still almost totally unknown.

General Gates placed his patriot army in position on Bemis Heights (near Saratoga) September 12, 1777. The next day Burgoyne's British troops crossed the Hudson, ready to attack. Two days later the German troops (helping the English) followed. By this time General Gates badly wanted to know how many guns and troops Burgoyne had. Most of all he wanted to know what Burgoyne was going to do next. He asked a local man named Alexander Bryan, whose home was somewhere near the American position, to go into Burgoyne's army and find out.

Bryan hesitated. He had a sick boy at home. His wife was just going to have a baby. General Gates promised to send an army doctor to take care of them. Being thus reassured and trusting to the general's promise, Bryan agreed to go.

To get safely in and out of the British lines, Bryan adopted what seems like a very queer

trick. But however queer it was, it worked. He
bought a piece of cloth, then wandered about
the British camp pretending he was looking for
a tailor. Apparently this odd excuse for being
there was good enough, for no one stopped him.
Bryan moved around within the British lines
until he had succeeded in learning the answers
to General Gates's questions, and started back
only when he found he had at last begun to
arouse suspicions.

As he made his way to safety, he was pursued,
and he escaped only after spending an hour in
the water of a neighboring creek, which, in
October in upstate New York, was very cold
indeed.

In the end, however, he made his way safely
back to General Gates with the news that
Burgoyne would attack Bemis Heights. The
British were met and repulsed. Burgoyne soon
surrendered.

Not until his return did poor Bryan discover
that Gates, who often treated people shabbily,
and for a time intrigued against Washington himself, had not sent the physician to Mrs. Bryan,
as he had promised. Bryan's sick boy had died.
His wife had suffered a premature confinement,
from which she nearly died too. Suspicious neighbors had added to her troubles. They thought
her husband had really gone over to the enemy.

The general explained his failure to send the doctor by saying that his own army needed twice as many medical men as they had. That may have been true, but Gates had made a promise that he should have kept.

Seldom can one see how far the influence of a single heroic deed may reach. If Bryan's warning really did make possible the victory at Bemis Heights, it was one of the most important pieces of military intelligence ever received by any general in any army in any war. For the victory at Bemis Heights in the end forced Burgoyne to surrender. That surrender weakened the British terribly. The French government, seeing the Americans could now win the war, joined us as allies. Their aid made victory certain. Perhaps America owes it all to Alexander Bryan, the spy whose name has been almost forgotten.

The Wiles of Washington

SEVENTEEN SEVENTY-SEVEN was a desperate year for the hard-pressed Americans, until the victory over Burgoyne in the autumn. And great as that victory was, the terrible "year of the three 7's" was followed by the equally desperate winter of 1777-78, when Washington's soldiers struggled for survival at Valley Forge.

But the intelligence service, which had by this time improved enormously, saved the situation. It may be too much to say that the spies alone saved the Continental Army. But it is certainly true that without spies Burgoyne might have won along the Hudson and Washington might have lost everything along the Delaware, before the Americans had even gone into camp at Valley Forge.

The tremendous successes of American intelligence in Philadelphia in 1777 are in sharp contrast with its failure in New York the year before. By the time the enemy had taken Philadelphia, however, the general had learned his lesson. He now knew how to run an intelligence service. He soon knew nearly as much about the British army's doings as General Howe himself. Secret reports from within the city came into American headquarters almost "every hour on the hour." And though a good many spies were caught and hanged during this period, they were all British.

American secret agents by this time understood the technique of the spy's dangerous trade. That was because Washington, in sending General Mifflin to Philadelphia, had ordered him to train his spies before putting them to work.

The success was due to General Washington's ability to learn from past mistakes. When Nathaniel Sackett's unknown woman spy reported from New York in late March (or the first few days of April, 1777) that the British meant to attack the Quaker city, Washington at once began to set up a spy system there. After General Mifflin had done the preliminary work, a brilliant and devoted young officer, Major John Clark, took over his task. Major Clark soon had the assistance of another devoted American spymaster, Captain Charles Craig. These two hung constantly on the very edge of the British outposts, while Colonel Elias Boudinot continued his work as intelligence officer with the American forces.

Just beyond the British outposts hovered Major Allan McLane and his cavalry, sometimes helping the spies, sometimes only scouting, but always with sharp eyes on anything the redcoats tried to do.

Captain Charles Craig was stationed at Frankford. Now part of Philadelphia, Frankford was then a village just beyond the city limits and outside the British lines. Spies could come out secretly to meet the captain there.

Major Clark rode back and forth, twenty to sixty miles a day in all weather. He wore out several horses. In the long run he wore out his own health too. Knowing the Tories were after him, he changed his living quarters frequently. As a result of these precautions, Clark was never captured.

For a while, local Tories, who knew the local patriots by sight, watched all the roads leading into Philadelphia. They were to warn the redcoats when anyone who might possibly be an American spy tried to enter the town. The high sheriff of the county, another Tory, also tried his hand at spy catching. But these efforts did the enemy very little good. Clark's spies, both men and women, came and went as they pleased, and reported almost every move the enemy made.

It was all completely secret. To this day there is no way of finding out who most of the Philadelphia spies were. One was an old woman. Others pretended to be farmers, sneaking black-market food to the enemy. Some were Philadelphia gentry, probably Quaker businessmen. One was right on board a British warship. Another was "intimately acquainted" with many British officers, and spent his time listening to any military secrets they might let slip.

The amount and accuracy of the secret intelligence Clark's spies thus collected in Philadelphia is amazing. So is the speed with which they smuggled it out of the city. The first spy's report from Philadelphia was on its way to the American general only a few days after the redcoats marched in. Fighting at the Battle of Germantown ended on October 4, 1777. By five o'clock on the morning of October 6 Major Clark was reporting British losses. By ten o'clock that same day he had a report from an American spy who had been chatting with General Howe during the battle. This man gave a more detailed report on British losses. A few weeks later a spy sent Washington a report on the number of soldiers in Howe's army.

When the British attacked Fort Mifflin October 22, 1777, Major Clark and his spies predicted the enemy would soon give up. General Washington, who didn't believe it, soon learned the spies were right.

The next time Howe was preparing to attack the American forts, the spies sent their warnings weeks in advance. Then, for a while secret reports about the attack simply poured into Washington's headquarters. Thus warned, the American troops slipped away from the two forts (which they could not possibly defend) in plenty of time. When Howe marched out to Darby, Pennsylvania, the Americans knew a day ahead of time that he was coming. And when Howe tried to capture Lafayette himself, a Philadelphia spy warned the Frenchman in time for him to save himself and his troops.

Major Clark and his daring group of Philadelphia spies did more than provide Washington with the correct information he needed. They also helped him plant in British headquarters incorrect information about the Americans, thus completely deceiving the enemy. They did this so cleverly that the British were utterly misled. They swallowed all, or almost all, of the deceitful stories General Washington and Major Clark thought up—and some of them were whoppers.

Everyone knows the story of the hatchet, the

cherry tree, and how George Washington could not tell a lie. So far as anyone can find out now, George Washington never did tell a lie—in time of peace, or in his own private interests. But in war, deceiving the enemy was his duty. He loved to make sure that anyone spying on his army got completely wrong "facts." He was very clever about it, too. And he probably rather enjoyed fooling the enemy. He thought up some amazing falsehoods, which the British eagerly believed.

General Washington had begun deceiving them early in 1777, when his army was still in Morristown. The Americans discovered a British spy at work in their camp. When a staff officer proposed to arrest the man, however, Washington gave orders to let him go right on spying. Better make friends with him. In other words, better make sure the enemy agent got plenty of information—all of it wrong. An American officer immediately began to cultivate the spy's acquaintance, and the two were soon on friendly terms.

Meantime, by the commander in chief's orders, every brigadier general in the Continental Army prepared a false report, exaggerating the strength of his troops. The combined figures made the Continental Army appear a great deal stronger than it really was. All these papers were "carelessly" left where the spy could get them. He stole them and disappeared.

General Howe was so completely fooled that when another of his spies brought correct reports, showing how weak the Americans really were, Howe threatened to hang the poor fellow. He accused him of bringing in false information!

Washington's little trick had important results, because the British, instead of attacking the American forces when they were weak, believed them much stronger than they really were and let them alone. At that time the American army had almost no fighting strength at all. A few false reports planted on a spy had won more than a battle.

At about the same time Colonel Elias Boudinot put a "double spy" to work. At the colonel's request, Washington himself provided false information for this man to carry to the enemy. In fact the commander in chief was so pleased with their little scheme that he told Colonel Boudinot to add any other false information he could think of. Only if Colonel Boudinot added any, Washington wanted a written copy. Then it might be possible to send another double spy to the British. Both men would "carry the same Tale," said Washington. If the British received false information from two apparently independent sources, they would be sure to believe it.

The general was not always satisfied to have his false information reach the enemy from only two sources. It was a favorite Washington trick to let it "leak" to several different spies, either double agents of his own or genuine British spies who didn't know they were being fooled. By the time British headquarters had the same stories—all of them false—from several different sources in different parts of the country, they would seem to confirm each other absolutely.

Once the general had a long conversation with a man who was, as Washington well knew, strongly suspected of being a Tory spy. He did not give this suspicious character any false information. This time George Washington didn't *tell* any lies. Instead, he just asked questions from which the Tory could draw his own conclusions! Washington spent a great deal of time asking about Long Island and Sandy Hook. He wanted the spy to think the Americans were going to attack New York City. But Washington did not intend to do anything of the sort. He was really going to march to Virginia. After a little checking up that night, Colonel Boudinot felt sure the enemy had already been given the subtle false news.

At least twice General Washington is known to have written out for other Tory spies doctored information he wanted the enemy to have.

Who's Got the Button?

THE GREATEST THING the Philadelphia spies
ever did for their country was to issue a series
of warnings to General Washington in the
first few days of December, 1777. This was a
critical moment in the war. The Americans had
been beaten in the Battle of Brandywine Creek in
September, and they had been beaten again at
Germantown in October. Washington then
camped his army at Whitemarsh, not far from
Philadelphia, where it rested, licking its wounds,
and waited for the next move.

Now General Howe, occupying Philadelphia,
planned to make a night march out of the city
and surprise the Americans. If the British had
been able to catch Washington napping, as they

hoped, they might have won the war then and there. It would have been the third complete defeat for the American army within a few weeks. It might easily have been the last battle of the war. Each time it looked as if the Americans had no chance.

But Howe had hardly begun to make plans for his attack before the American spy system began to pour information in upon the commander in chief at Whitemarsh. Each independent report confirmed the others. On December 1 Washington heard from Major Clark: "Orders were given to the [British] troops to hold themselves in readiness to march." Next day Captain Charles Craig, at Frankford, a few miles away, sent word that the enemy intended "to drive your Excellency from the present encampment." Five hundred redcoats had crossed the Schuylkill River. The next day, December 3, Craig reported again. Three thousand British troops had now crossed the river to strike the Americans in their rear. At one o'clock Major Clark sent the information: "The enemy are in motion, have a number of flat-bottomed boats and carriages." They were taking horses and wagons from farmers. "In motion" did not necessarily mean that the British were already marching; it did mean they were preparing a military operation of some kind. At six o'clock Clark sent in another report. It was ac-

curate, last-minute military intelligence. Major
Clark had received it from an American spy who
had left Philadelphia at noon. The British troops
had received orders to hold themselves in readiness. They were to draw two days' rations. Biscuit
was being served out to them when the spy left.
At the last moment one more warning came in
from Captain Allan McLane, reconnoitering with
his cavalry: "An attempt to surprise the American camp at White Marsh was about to be
made."

Meantime, a quiet Philadelphia housewife was
surpassing the whole secret service, from within
the enemy's most secret councils. This daring
volunteer spy was Mrs. Lydia Darragh. Since
she was a Quaker, we really ought to call her
"Friend Darragh," not "Mrs. Darragh."

Almost opposite her house, which was then
Number 177 on the east side of Second Street,
stood the house that had at first been the headquarters of General Howe himself and was now
the headquarters of a German general, his ally.

Notwithstanding the fact that she was a
Quaker, Friend Lydia Darragh was a stanch and
active patriot. She had good reason to wish for
an American victory. Her son Charles was a
lieutenant in General Washington's camp at
Whitemarsh.

Friend Lydia may have been one of Major

Clark's spies. It is more likely that she was operating a little system of her own within the family. She herself collected the information. Her husband copied her reports, in shorthand, on bits of paper small enough to be folded and hidden inside large button molds. She then covered the wooden button molds with the cloth that matched her younger son John's suit, and sewed them on the jacket. This fourteen-year-old boy, an important courier now, slipped off to the American camp, wearing his suit with its cloth buttons. His older brother, Lieutenant Charles, removed the messages from the buttons. Charles, who could read his father's shorthand, transcribed the messages for George Washington.

As time drew near for the planned attack, the enemy unconsciously played into Lydia Darragh's hands. Requiring more rooms, their billeting officer ordered her husband to turn over his house to the British army, "and find other quarters for his family." The Quaker mother (who had originally come from Ireland) was incensed. She marched across the street to protest at headquarters.

Now, serving with the British was one Captain Barrington, and he may have been the officer to whom Lydia protested. He may also have been her kinsman from the old country, for her maiden name had been Barrington. Moreover, the captain may also have known her schoolmaster husband, who had once been private tutor in the Barrington family in Ireland. This may be the reason that the British changed their demands. They said that the Darraghs could stay in their own house if they would let General Howe have one room for a council chamber.

Lydia gave the British a room at the back of the house, upstairs, and sent her younger children to the country. She kept John, the fourteen-year-old, at home. He was going to be needed.

Busy officers in scarlet began to pass in and out of her house constantly. There was much conferring in the Darragh's back room. (The British could not have known that the Quaker Darragh family had a son serving with the patriots at Whitemarsh, for they would naturally suppose that, as Quakers, the Darraghs were taking no part in the war.)

On December 2, 1777, several days after Major Clark's spies had begun to warn the Continental Army, a British officer ordered Lydia Darragh to send her family to bed early that night. The staff wished to use the room for an important conference, and they must be free from interruption. Officers would begin to arrive about seven.

After providing candles for light and wood to keep the hearth fire going, the Darraghs dutifully retired. Early that winter evening British officers began to arrive.

Lydia Darragh could not sleep. Years later, remembering that anxious night, she told her daughter that "a presentiment of evil weighed down her spirits." She knew this secret consultation boded ill for the American camp, where her son lay sleeping, within easy striking distance. She could hear the hum of enemy voices. It was more than she could endure.

She slipped into a little closet adjoining the conference room. Here the wall was only a thin board partition covered with wallpaper, and she could hear every word they said.

Lydia Darragh had let her eavesdropping go until almost too late. The officers were now getting ready to leave, but one of them read aloud a paper that summed up the decisions they had made. Imagine her holding her breath while she listened to that voice!

The British would march out of Philadelphia by night on December 4. They would surprise Washington's army at Whitemarsh. With their superior force and the unprepared condition of the unsuspecting Americans, their victory was certain.

With palpitating heart, Friend Darragh hurried back to bed and pretended to be sound asleep. The conference broke up. She could hear chairs scraping over the floor, then a rattling of swords. There was the sound of heavy boots walking toward her bedroom door, a sharp tap, and then an officer called out that they were going now. She should lock up the house and see to the fire and candles. Clever Lydia made no reply.

The officer knocked louder. He called louder, until finally he heard her sleepy-sounding response. He later remembered that she had seemed very sleepy.

It took the distraught mother all next day (December 3) to decide what to do. It might not be easy now to pass the British outguards. They would be tightening up their precautions as they prepared to march. She would need a pretext, and it would have to be a good one. According to one version of the story, she pretended to be going to see her children in the country. According to another, she pretended to be on her way to get flour from a mill at Frankford. Both tales were plausible, and she probably told both.

But to her husband she said nothing. She merely announced that she was going to use a British pass, which she possessed, to go out into the country. This time she would not be needing his shorthand, for she was going herself. This errand was too important to entrust to anyone

else, and the whole report was in her own head;
it need not be written down.

Lydia Darragh's unwillingness to confide in
her husband may have been because she feared
he might try to stop her from undertaking such a
risk. As it was, he is said to have been surprised
because she did not take her maid with her.

Once more fortune favored the brave. Lydia
Darragh had some hardships, but no interference.
On the morning of December 4 she was trudging
along the road running northeast from Philadelphia to the mill on Frankford Creek. British outposts let her proceed. Why not? Her dress showed
she was a Friend. She had General Howe's pass.
Besides, her errand seemed quite natural. Phila-
delphians were in the habit of walking out of town
to the flour mills near the city. To make it all
seem plausible, Lydia Darragh carried an empty
flour bag. A small and rather frail woman, no
longer young, hardly seemed dangerous. Let her
through!

By the time she reached Frankford, she was
outside the British-held terrain. Leaving her bag
at the mill to be filled, she turned westward along
Nice Town Lane, toward the Rising Sun Tavern,
kept by the Widow Nice.

She had taken the right direction. Somewhere
in that vicinity Major Allan McLane's patriot
cavalry patrols were covering the American de-

fense lines around the camp at Whitemarsh. Major Benjamin Tallmadge was also out on reconnaissance. During the morning Colonel Elias Boudinot had gone as far forward as the Rising Sun Tavern, a few miles west of Frankford Mill. Here the Americans had a small outpost. After dining, the colonel had remained there, using it as a message center. Probably Colonel Thomas Craig, mounted, well acquainted with the locality, was also keeping an eye on what passed along Nice Town Lane. And Captain Charles Craig was at his post in Frankford, not far away. The American army already had its "feelers" out.

Of course Friend Darragh could not know it, but General Washington had already had three or four days' warning of the contemplated British surprise, and was taking all precautions. His intelligence men were on the alert. McLane had drawn a cavalry screen, as well as he could, with his few troopers. The Americans had posted a line of observers for several miles across all possible enemy approaches. With an attack imminent, the place for the army intelligence was well forward, and that is where Colonel Boudinot was stationed, just behind the cavalry. His task was to receive and evaluate information as soon as received—not to go scouting himself. Events proved that this was the right course of action.

Plodding steadily along, Lydia Darragh presently met an American officer. Probably this was Colonel Thomas Craig. Any unexplained civilians going down Nice Town Lane from the east were sure to be stopped for questioning on that particular morning. Craig, a Pennsylvanian who knew the Darragh family, was surprised to see this respectable Philadelphia matron trudging down the wintry lane, between two armies.

"Why, Mrs. Darragh," he is supposed to have asked, "what are you doing so far from home?"

Leading his horse, he walked along beside her while she gave him her news. After pausing long enough to take the tired woman into a farmhouse and make sure she got some food, Colonel Craig hurried the vital message back to General Washington, according to one version of the story.

It seems, however, that Lydia Darragh, afraid that Craig might not get the information back in time, sent her report in a second way:

Colonel Boudinot was still in the Rising Sun Tavern that afternoon when a woman came in and began to talk to him. This was probably not Lydia Darragh, however, but a woman sent by her. Boudinot later described this woman as "a little, poor-looking, insignificant old woman." Ann Darragh, Lydia's daughter who told the story of her mother's exploits, said her mother was "of a fair complexion, light hair, blue eyes, very delicate in appearance and extremely neat; conforming in her dress to the Society of Friends."

As this does not fit Boudinot's description, it seems likely that when Lydia Darragh was in the farmhouse where Craig had taken her, she put her message in writing and sent it on to the American colonel by some other woman. The sooner she herself was back in Philadelphia, the fewer questions would be asked.

At any rate, after the strange woman talked with Colonel Boudinot in the Rising Sun Tavern, she handed him "a dirty old needlebook, with various small pockets in it." (Lydia Darragh, known for her neatness, would hardly be carrying a "dirty" old needlebook. This, no doubt, was something she picked up at the farmhouse.) The surprised colonel took the little needlebook.

Then he examined the little packet: "I could not find anything till I got to the last pocket, where I found a piece of paper rolled up into the form of a pipe shank. On unrolling it I found information that General Howe was coming out the next morning with 5000 men, 13 pieces of cannon, baggage wagons, and 11 boats on wheels" —the latter being pontoon-bridge equipment.

Hurrying back to headquarters, Boudinot went at once to General Washington. He made his report in the way Washington had ordered—facts only, "without comment or opinion."

Washington listened silently. When Boudinot finished, the general said nothing. He merely sat there, thinking.

Colonel Boudinot decided to risk expressing a few opinions after all. He couldn't forget those eleven boats on wheels. They meant, he told Washington, that the enemy was going to pretend to cross the Delaware into New Jersey. Then their soldiers would cross into Pennsylvania again and smash into the undefended rear of the Continental Army. Still the commander in chief just sat there, thinking.

Colonel Boudinot repeated his opinion. When he still received no reply, he repeated it a third time. At last the tall man in the blue and buff uniform with the three silver stars on his shoulders roused himself. No, he told the colonel, the enemy would not attack the American rear. They were taking boats along just to fool any American spies who might see them. General Howe would attack the American left. Washington even said which road he would use.

Poor Boudinot felt sure his commander in chief was all wrong. He told some of the officers the enemy was sure to attack the rear next morning. The Americans were sure to lose their baggage train.

The British moved out of Philadelphia at eleven
o'clock on the night of December 4, probably
with a good many more men than the five thousand Lydia Darragh had reported. They kept
wagons and field artillery rolling through the city
all night, in the wrong direction, as if they were
heading for the Schuylkill River. It was a clever
trick, but Major Allan McLane was not deceived.

At three o'clock in the morning there was a
crash of alarm guns on the very road by which
General Washington said the enemy would come
that night—the road on which Colonel Boudinot
was sleeping! Though he himself had thought
his general was making the wrong estimate, he
had ordered a picket posted down the road and
all horses to be kept saddled, just in case!

When the guns boomed, Boudinot and the
others with him rode for their lives. By dawn the
redcoats were already occupying the quarters
where the skeptical Boudinot had been sleeping.
Washington had been right. Boudinot later admitted ruefully, "I then said that I never would
again set up my judgment against his."

Washington, forewarned by Clark and Craig
as well as Lydia Darragh, had kept the American
troops busy strengthening their positions—in
front, not in the rear. The British "surprise" had
failed. Everywhere, the Continental Army was
deployed, entrenched, grimly waiting.

The two armies sat glaring at each other all day long. The British reconnoitered, but could find no soft spots. General Howe, who had led the redcoats to slaughter on Bunker Hill, knew better now than to try a frontal assault on entrenched Americans. Their aim was too deadly. British General "No Flint" Grey had a brush with Morgan's and Gist's riflemen, which cost a hundred British lives. Otherwise the two forces merely looked at each other all day long.

At noon next day General Howe gave up. The British army marched back to Philadelphia, "like a parcel of damned fools," as one of its disgusted officers said. It was a magnificent example of what a few really good spies and some wide-awake cavalry scouts could accomplish.

The Whitemarsh fiasco greatly discouraged the British. When Cornwallis, who left Philadelphia for a short leave in England, reported on the failure at Whitemarsh in London, he added that the conquest of America was impossible. General Washington now seemed to the British like a sly fox no one could catch.

To British headquarters in Philadelphia it was painfully apparent that there had been a leak somewhere. An impressive figure in scarlet and gold, topped with a serious face, summoned the demure Lydia Darragh in her Quaker gray to the conference room. The dauntless lady told her family afterward that, but for the darkness, he would have guessed what she had done because she was so pale.

The solemn-looking officer in the brilliant uniform locked the door behind him. Had any of the Darragh family been awake on the night the officers had conferred?

"No, they were all in bed and asleep."

"I need not ask you," said the officer, "for we had great difficulty in waking you to fasten the door after us. But one thing is certain: the enemy had notice of our coming."

The lady used to recall with satisfaction that she "never told a lie about it. I could answer all his questions without that," she said. She told her exciting story to her daughter Ann, who wrote it down. But for Ann, we should not know of the brave exploit of that one particular Philadelphia housewife.

Of course, brave or not, what she and her soldier son did was not according to the rules of Friends. Some years later, the Friends' meeting to which the Darraghs belonged cast out Lieutenant Charles Darragh for "engaging in matters of a warlike nature," and his mother for "neglecting to attend our religious meetings." They never knew that she had helped to prevent a battle and to shorten the war, with its death and suffering.

IV. Super Spies, 1778-1781

The Culpers' Secret Ink

AFTER WHITEMARSH, General Washington moved his army to Valley Forge, where it struggled through a long hard winter, while the British made themselves comfortable in Philadelphia. General Sir William Howe, aware that he had failed to crush the rebellion, resigned his command and sailed back to England. He announced his intended departure May 11, 1778. (Washington had the news from his spies two days later.)

Washington's main problem after that was to find out what General Sir Henry Clinton, the new British commander in chief, meant to do. All reports indicated Clinton would evacuate Philadelphia. But then what?

If Clinton did evacuate, he could do only three things: (1) He could admit the British were

beaten and give up the thirteen American
colonies entirely, trying to save only the West
Indian and Canadian colonies. The war showed
signs of spreading. France and Spain were grow-
ing hostile. They might declare war on King
George at any moment—as in fact they eventually
did. If, however, Clinton meant to try to hold
the American colonies, there were still two
courses he could take. (2) He could take his
army to New York by water. Or (3) he could
march to New York overland, through New
Jersey.

For a little while General Washington really
had hopes the enemy might give up the war.
Then spies' reports began to indicate that Clinton
meant to withdraw to New York. At the end of
May a fleet of a hundred ships sailed from Philadelphia. A spy in Chester, Pennsylvania, watched
it go. Allan McLane's cavalry rode near enough
to see that Philadelphia Harbor was *almost*
empty. Reports from New York showed that the
staff there were getting ready to quarter more
British troops. Then spies and coast watchers
reported the fleet had actually arrived in New
York Harbor, but apparently brought no army
with it, only Tory refugees and army supplies.

A vigilant watch was kept. Clinton and his
redcoats were all still in Philadelphia. The fleet
had carried baggage and fleeing Tories only. Gen-

eral Washington was sure now there would be a move through New Jersey. With the ships gone, there was no other way.

The Philadelphia spies, still keeping a close watch on the redcoats, began to report the enemy was busily collecting flat-bottomed boats. That meant they would cross the Delaware. They were also collecting horses and wagons. They would be used to carry baggage across New Jersey. It was now clear that Clinton would march from Philadelphia to New York.

As usual, General Washington was right. Within three weeks Clinton was doing just what the American commander had expected. Because it possessed all this advance intelligence, the Continental Army was ready to pursue the redcoats when the time came.

There was a little delay at first, because the Philadelphia spies were slow in reporting the first British move. General Washington had no word that the enemy was actually marching away until Philadelphia had been wholly evacuated, on June 18.

Clinton had slipped his army out of Philadelphia on the night of June 17–18. His entire force was across the river by 10 A.M. on the eighteenth. Clinton himself had spent the early morning hours sitting on a rock, ready to take personal command against an American attack that never

came, though Sir Henry fully expected it. For
once the Philadelphia spies had blundered. They
had not given Washington a chance to catch
Clinton with his forces divided by the river. The
American command knew nothing about the
move till almost noon.

Espionage on Manhattan and Long Island now
became more important for the Americans.
Colonel Elias Dayton's spies had long been operating in New York, but more intelligence was
now needed. Through the summer of 1778 more
networks were formed. General Charles Scott
began to set up an intelligence service covering
Long Island and New York City. He used a small
group of resident secret agents, who never left
the islands, but sent out information through a
regular system of secret couriers.

By the end of the summer, Major Benjamin
Tallmadge, of the Second Connecticut Dragoons,
began to take over the work General Scott had
started. The organization Scott and Tallmadge
set up was a model of its kind. It provided abund-
ant, accurate, detailed, and valuable information
in absolute secrecy. It went right on till the end of
the war without detection. The Americans even
kept a horse for the spies' use behind the British
lines. General Washington paid the bills!

The two principal agents of this network were
known as "the Culpers," a secret code name

meant to conceal their real identities. Samuel Woodhull, of Setauket, Long Island, operated under the code name of "Culper Sr." Robert Townsend of New York City was "Culper Jr."

Woodhull's main task was receiving and transmitting the intelligence Townsend collected in New York. Sometimes he personally observed British headquarters, personnel, troops, supplies, and fortifications on Long Island. He also reported what he could see in New York City on occasional visits. For excellent reasons, he made such visits as few as possible, never more than would seem perfectly natural.

As a spy, Woodhull's colleague, Robert Townsend, had three great advantages. Townsend was a New York merchant. As a merchant, he frequently had to deliver goods on Long Island. That made his communication with Woodhull (Culper Sr.) entirely natural. A second advantage was that his father lived at Oyster Bay, Long Island. That gave him another good excuse for leaving New York City and visiting Long Island. A third advantage was that he was an amateur dabbler in journalism, writing for the New York *Gazette*. The *Gazette* was a violently Tory paper, published by the notoriously pro-British printer, James Rivington. Townsend was careful to give all the news stories he wrote a fiercely Tory, anti-American slant.

So well did these men keep their secret that not till nearly a hundred and fifty years had passed did anyone guess who the Culpers really were. And not till 1959 was it finally proved that Rivington, the supposed Tory, was really another American secret agent. His greatest achievement as a spy was stealing the British Navy's signal book. Washington, who had no navy to speak of, sent it on to the French Admiral de Grasse.

As Rivington's reporter, it was natural for Townsend (Culper Jr.) to frequent the coffeehouse that the Tory publisher operated, partly as a profitable side line, partly as a useful place to pick up news. In the relaxing social life of the coffeehouse, in the unimpeachably royalist atmosphere that Rivington maintained in conversation with the Tory's own newswriter, it was natural that king's officers should talk freely. It was an ideal arrangement for the Americans.

If Culper Sr. happened to visit New York when intelligence was ready, Culper Jr. gave it to him orally. Culper Sr. took it home in his head and wrote it down after he was safely back in Setauket. Otherwise Culper Jr. turned his reports over to a courier, Austin Roe, who made the fifty-mile ride to Setauket ostensibly with merchandise. As a precaution, courier Roe did not stop at Culper Sr.'s house at all, but left the messages in a box buried in an open field.

Though the British held all of Long Island and all of New York City, the Americans held the whole Connecticut coast across Long Island Sound opposite Long Island. At Stamford, Connecticut, was Lieutenant Caleb Brewster. He was in the army now, but had served aboard a whaling ship. With his experience as a sailor, Brewster was the ideal army officer to command the specially picked crew who took a whaleboat secretly across Long Island Sound, landed by night on Long Island, and got the spies' reports from Woodhull. When Brewster returned to Connecticut, he turned the papers over to Major Benjamin Tallmadge. The major had cavalrymen ready to rush them off full speed to General Washington's headquarters.

Everything was handled with the deepest secrecy. Washington dealt with most of the reports personally. The only one of his staff officers known ever to have handled these precious reports was Captain Alexander Hamilton—later a great figure in American political affairs. Once General Washington expressed a wish to meet one of the Culpers and give personal instructions. But when he was told how dangerous this would be for the spy, he gave up the idea. Washington never even saw most of his best helpers in the secret service.

At first the Culpers worked in dread that captured messages would reveal what they were

doing. They were sending their reports in plain
English, uncoded and unciphered. They were
also writing in ordinary ink. This was much too
dangerous. They were soon given a fairly good
code in which numbers were used for important
words. To make their messages more secret still,
John Jay's brother, Sir James Jay, supplied a
secret ink. Sir James had been a doctor, practic-
ing in England. As a medical man, he had learned
enough chemistry to invent an invisible ink,
which left no mark on paper until another chemical was brushed on the paper. Sir James's inven-
tion was variously known as "white," "sympathetic," "invisible," and "secret" ink. Washington and the Culpers usually called it "stain."

The two Jay brothers knew the ink was good,
for they had been using it in private correspondence for several years. Then someone realized
how valuable it would be to the American army.
General Washington first mentioned it in a letter
to Major Tallmadge, April 30, 1779. The general,
who had just heard of it, had not been able to
get any of the magic fluid. Three days later he
wrote Colonel Dayton: "It is in my power, I believe, to procure a liquid which nothing but a
counter liquor (rubbed over the paper after-
wards) can make legible." By the end of May the
Culpers were using the secret ink, but it was a
one-way correspondence, for, as a precaution,

the spies never had any of the developer. They could write their messages in the secret ink. If the British raided the spies' rooms, they still would not be able to read the secret messages. There would be no developer there to capture.

At first, Culper Jr. simply sent his information in secret ink on what looked like blank sheets of paper. Even that was dangerous. If such paper were ever captured, the enemy would at once become suspicious, especially after the British did capture a letter in ordinary ink referring to the invisible ink. They now knew the Americans were using invisible writing. The British had two secret inks of their own, one developed by heat, the other by an acid. It might not be difficult for the British to develop Sir James Jay's chemical, if they captured letters written in it. To avoid this risk, General Washington suggested that Culper Jr. should occasionally write his information on the blank leaves of a pamphlet or "an almanack" or a cheap little book.

A few months later General Washington made another suggestion. The blank paper, he pointed out, was "sufficient to raise suspicion." He suggested that the spy write a letter commenting on family matters, with Tory sentiments. Then the spy was to write his message with invisible ink between the lines and on the empty margins.

The Culpers themselves hit upon a third

method of avoiding suspicion. It was natural for Culper Jr., as a merchant, to be sending packages of blank paper along with other merchandise to his Long Island customers. He began to write his invisible message on one blank sheet. This he inserted among the other sheets. No matter to whom these packages were addressed, they went first to Culper Sr., who had previously been given a number by Culper Jr.—say, twenty-five. Culper Sr. counted through the sheets until he came to number twenty-five, which he took out. This sheet he sent on, still blank, to Major Tallmadge. Tallmadge had the developer and brought the secret message to light.

Later Culper Jr. had a fourth useful idea. He began to write occasional short business letters to some of his customers, always selecting well-known Tories. On the blank part of each sheet he put his secret message in Jay's "stain." If these letters were intercepted, they would not look suspicious. Culper Jr. was a prominent New York businessman. He was supposed to be a Tory. It was natural for a well-known Tory businessman to be writing a business letter to a well-known Tory customer.

But one thing was important: the courier had to be careful these letters never reached the persons to whom they were addressed! None of them ever did.

Major Tallmadge added both cipher and code to the precautions protecting his secret papers. The cipher was of the ordinary substitution type, such as Dr. Church had used. But Culper Jr. did not have to rely solely on secret ink and cipher. Tallmadge also made a small dictionary in numbered code, although he was foolish enough to number the words in their alphabetical order, with very little variation. According to his scheme, word numbers ran like this:

> they — 629
> there — 630
> thing — 631
> though — 632
> time — 633
> to — 634
> troops — 635

and so forth. This meant that words in *a* had low numbers—"advice" was 15. Words toward the end of the alphabet had high numbers—"zeal" being 710. This might have made possible the breaking of the code, but fortunately that never happened.

Important place names and individuals had separate numbers, and these Tallmadge did not put in alphabetical order. General Washington was 711; Tallmadge, 721; Culper Sr. (Woodhull), 722; Culper Jr. (Townsend), 723; New York, 727; Long Island, 728; Setauket, 729.

Major Tallmadge made three code books—one for himself, one for Culper Jr., and one for General Washington. There may have been a fourth for Culper Sr., but no more. These books were dangerous. Were a spy caught with one in his possession, that alone would convict him.

The Culpers had several narrow escapes from discovery. The British soon knew that there was a leak somewhere. Perhaps this was because their own counterespionage was active. Perhaps it was because they so often found General Washington so surprisingly well informed so far ahead of time. Once Culper Sr. was stopped and searched at the Brooklyn Ferry. He was even told that "some villain" was sending information to the rebels. Since the inspectors failed to find the reports of Culper Jr., which he—the very "villain" they were after—was at that moment carrying, he was passed through. General Washington got his intelligence, but it was a tight squeak and a harrowing moment for Woodhull.

His worst fright of the war occurred once while he was writing with his secret ink in his bedroom, nervously aware that several British officers were quartered in the next chamber. Suddenly the door burst open. He leaped to his feet in terror, snatched at his papers, upset his table, spilled his priceless fluid, and whirled around—

all in an instant—to behold two playful young women who just wanted to surprise him!

Riding from the city to his home in Setauket, Woodhull was once held up and searched by four bandits. As he had only a dollar in cash, they let him go. They never guessed he had secret papers inside his saddle. The highwaymen may have been ordinary criminals, taking advantage of the disorder of the times. But if they had found the papers, they could have taken Woodhull to Sir Henry Clinton and received a reward for exposing a spy. Twice British foragers came near the home of this devoted agent. He reported, "Their coming was like death to me." Once his home was raided, but he was away at the time.

The Culpers' most important achievement was thwarting Sir Henry Clinton's move to interfere with the French, arriving at Newport to aid the American cause, in the summer of 1779. When the French troops landed in July, the British secret courier bringing the news into New York City was riding just a little way behind the Culpers' courier, Austin Roe. Like all troops disembarking, the French were in a state of temporary confusion, and it was just the moment for the British to jump on them. Austin Roe was waiting on Manhattan Island while Townsend (Culper Jr.) finished his report, showing that Clinton was starting to move his troops. Never had a warning to General Washington been more urgent. Never had Culper Jr. so feared discovery. The British were now stopping everyone who might possibly carry information about their movements. Roe must appear innocent.

The spy did not want to burden his courier with the usual letter, hidden in the ream of blank paper. If Austin Roe carried one such package, he would have to carry others. A single parcel would look suspicious. Many packages meant weight; weight meant delay, slowing down the horse. Austin Roe's message was urgent. He could not delay.

This time, instead of sending a package, Culper Jr. wrote a letter to a well-known Long Island Tory, one Colonel Floyd. Having recently been robbed, Floyd would naturally be buying things. The message was in ordinary ink. It simply said, "The articles you want cannot be procured; as soon as they can will send them." Of course Roe never delivered this letter to Floyd. It went to General Washington's headquarters with its hidden message. But if Roe had been caught and searched, the message would have seemed innocent enough. Roe covered the fifty miles to Setauket by evening, in time to send the word across Long Island Sound. Meantime Sir Henry Clinton's troops were beginning to move.

General Washington managed to have some

"secret papers" accidentally "captured." He had
no idea at all of attacking Clinton in New York.
His army was not strong enough. But the secret
papers he wanted captured, for Clinton to see,
said plainly that the Americans meant to make
an offensive movement against Manhattan Island.
The clever ruse worked. Clinton stayed; his
British troops disembarked again, and in Newport the French were undisturbed. Culper Jr.'s
timely intelligence had prevented an attack.

To the end of the war the Culpers' flow of information continued. They gave news of arrival
and departure of British ships, British morale,
British losses in action, warning against British
agents in the American lines, movements of
British generals, exact location of individual
units of the enemy and of their quartermaster
supplies. They supplied maps and position
sketches. This steady flow of accurate information
kept General Washington in touch at all times
with enemy activity.

The Culpers could not have done it without
Caleb Brewster and his Connecticut and Long
Island crews, who ran several whaleboats, based
at Fairfield, back and forth across Long Island
Sound. These crews were natives of Long Island
or Connecticut. Some of them, like Joshua Davis,
had been withdrawn from the infantry for this
special service.

The romantic aspects of secret service were doubled for Joshua, who was then in his early twenties. In the midst of his mysterious comings and goings he met and married eighteen-year-old Abigail Redfield in Fairfield. She was often lonely during her husband's absences and used to drop in at a neighbor's for comfort. Long after the war the woman she visited explained that Davis' wife complained of being lonesome because her husband "was absent a considerable part of the time under Capt. Brewster." Everyone in Fairfield seems to have known about Brewster and his "spy boat." So did the British, but they could never catch him.

These courageous men contributed a great deal to winning the war. It is possible that without the military intelligence they gave the commander in chief, the war could not have been won at all. But their names do not appear in the history books. For a long time after the Revolution no one even knew who they were. Even today few people except a small group of historical specialists know anything about them. The Culpers and their friends did the dangerous work of the secret service. The secret service keeps silent when its work is done. It expects no notice, no credit, no fame, and no reward—and, it doesn't get any, either! For such men, the nation's safety is reward enough.

The Tricky Double Agents

THE DOUBLE AGENT, the man who spies for both sides, is the one who is hardest to trust. The officers who use him always wonder whether he has any loyalty at all. Is he loyal to one side? If so, which side is it? Sometimes a double agent really does spy for both sides, selling information cheerfully for all the money he can get, caring not a bit about either side. But there were few, if any, such scoundrels in the American Revolution. Various men pretended to be spying for the British when they were really loyal American secret agents. We can be sure of this today, because the secret papers of both armies have now been opened. Possibly a few of the men who seemed to be spying for the Americans were really spying for the British. But they don't show

up in the secret-service manuscripts that have
come down to us.

No one knows who all the genuinely patriotic
double agents were—that is, the men who pretended to be British spies but were sincerely
working for American victory. Some of the men
who carried over to the British the false information General Washington and Major John Clark
wanted the British to have were certainly genuine
British spies. There were several secret agents
whom the Americans knew all about. Washington
let them keep on spying, because he could use
them to plant false papers. These men just didn't
know they were being used to deceive the army
of their king.

The names of only three of General Washington's double agents are known. These were perfectly loyal American officers who really spied
for Washington and only pretended to spy for
the enemy: Captains Elijah Hunter, David Gray,
and Caleb Bruen. There were certainly other
double spies in or around Philadelphia. Probably there were a great many more.

One of the most successful of these double
agents was Captain Elijah Hunter. Living at
Bedford, in Westchester County, just outside
New York City, it was easy for him to make his
way in and out as the occasion required. Captain
Hunter had "retired" from the Second New York

Militia in 1776. No one knows why, but it is possible he had already begun to spy for John Jay in 1778. He was known as a trusty patriot by General Alexander McDougall, as the year 1779 began. In early February the general told Captain Hunter and two other men, of whom nothing is known, to make friends with the British. The general wanted them all "to enter deeply in correspondence with the enemy"—to pretend they were traitors. Nothing is known about the others, but Hunter fooled the British so completely that he had soon won the confidence not only of General Sir Henry Clinton but also of William Tryon, the Tory governor of New York.

Hunter worked so fast that in March he came back from New York with a great deal of useful military information. He had been having a confidential talk with Clinton and Tryon, who, thinking him a trustworthy Tory, told him to leave the city, pose as a patriot, and spy on the Americans. He had been an American spy to begin with. It was the British themselves who made him into a double spy. Tryon himself asked Captain Hunter to work into a position of trust among the patriots, then visit Washington's headquarters as a spy, and at the same time to act like a zealous American so as not to shake the confidence of his countrymen. Hunter dutifully reported all this to the American general, Alexander

McDougall, who promptly sent him on to Washington.

Though Hunter arrived with a recommenda-
tion from that veteran spy catcher, John Jay, General Washington did not at first trust him. He
admitted that Hunter looked like "a sensible man
capable of rendering important services." But
was he "sincerely disposed?" It was always
"necessary to be very circumspect with double
spies," said the general, which sounds as if he
had already used a good many of them. Besides,
although Hunter had turned in, for Washington's
examination, a letter addressed to Sir Frederick
Haldimand, British commander in Canada, that
did not *prove* his good faith in the eyes of the
suspicious American commander in chief. General Washington thought the letter looked as if
"intended to fall into our hands." He suspected
Hunter might be "as much in interest of the
enemy as in ours"—the usual trouble with double
spies.

But Hunter kept turning in so much information that by September Washington "had not the
smallest doubt of his attachment and integrity."
Hunter even managed to steal a letter of the
British cavalry raider, Colonel Banastré Tarleton.
He sent this to Washington to read. But he insisted it must be returned to him. Evidently he
intended to replace it in Tarleton's file before

its loss was discovered. There must have been some good reason why he didn't simply copy it himself. Probably he wanted Washington to see it in Tarleton's own handwriting.

When Hunter asked for information of the American army which he could supply to the British, Washington gave him correct information—if it was harmless and there was no objection to letting the British know it. He also provided false information.

Into this web of deceit the Americans wove a new strand of double-dyed imposture in the winter of 1779–80. This was the handiwork of Captain David Gray, a Massachusetts Yankee, one of the most successful double agents in history. Gray, who already held an American commission, first persuaded the enemy to take him into their secret service. Then, for nearly two years, he went in and out of New York whenever he wished, casually betraying Tories along the way and obligingly pausing in his errands for Sir Henry Clinton to tell General Washington all about Sir Henry's doings.

At least once Captain Gray did give the British information about America's French allies, but it was only information they would get anyhow. Probably he gave information about Washington's troops too—the chance to plant false information was too good for General Washing-

ton to miss. Since we can now read the British
secret-service reports, it is clear Gray never gave
away any American or French information that
mattered. Of course he had to give the British
some information, or he would have come under
suspicion.

Captain Gray's career as a double agent began
when he was transferred to the quartermasters
and sent on a supply mission to Lake George and
New Hampshire. Here he accidentally discovered
a chain of Tories. He soon found it reached from
Canada to Rope Ferry, near New London, Connecticut. This discovery stirred his first interest
in secret service. Ordered back from New Hampshire with dispatches, he visited Continental
headquarters, whence he was sent to Lieutenant
Colonel William Ledyard at New London.
Probably he was carrying a message warning the
colonel about the Tories. Overtaken by darkness,
Gray put up at an inn five miles from New London and fell into company with a British captain.
(Gray spelled his name Beckit, but he may have
been Captain George Beckwith, of Sir Henry
Clinton's staff.) Gray soon found that the British
officer, whoever he was, was secretly collecting
information about the American army and taking
it to New York. Gray probably gained the man's
confidence by talking as if he, too, were a member of a Tory spy network. He could have made

his story sound truthful, since he already knew a good deal about what the New England Tories were secretly doing. At any rate, the British captain accepted the American captain as a genuine turncoat and agreed to take him to Long Island the next night.

In the morning, before the pair started for the British lines, Gray proceeded to New London, five miles away, where he delivered his message to American Lieutenant Colonel Ledyard. Then, with his new British "friend," he started for Long Island and New York City.

The supposed deserter went at once to the Tory intelligence officer, Colonel Beverly Robinson, on whose lands Gray's father had once been a tenant. Then he went to see a Tory named John Cane, in Brooklyn. Next day Cane took him back to Colonel Robinson. All three agreed that, as Gray had a commission in Washington's army, it would be easy for him to carry British secret messages anywhere he wanted. (It *was* easy, too. General Washington saw to that!)

Captain Gray was given secret British dispatches for the first time. He dutifully delivered them and dutifully returned with the answers. He must have known the British were testing him out. Presently he was sent again, with more letters, to Vermont and New Hampshire. This time, as soon as he was safely off the island, he opened some of these official missives. Seeing that they would be useful to General Washington, he went immediately to him.

The general asked how he got them. Gray explained he had been in New York, had "joined" the British secret service, and was likely to obtain further intelligence. Washington gave back the letters, told him to deliver them, provided some money and what Gray called an "elegant horse." He also supplied a pass, signed by his own hand, which allowed Gray to move about unmolested and to cross the Sound into British lines. After that, Gray stayed in the British secret service until 1782, but always as a loyal American agent in constant touch with Washington.

Once Gray's true loyalty to America made him forget the part he was "acting." While on his way from New York to Canada, carrying an important message from the Tory Major Oliver DeLancey to General Sir Guy Carleton in September, 1781, he stopped in New London and turned the enemy's papers over to Lieutenant Colonel William Ledyard, who sent them on to Washington. He also warned Ledyard that the traitor Benedict Arnold was assembling his Tory "Legion" at Huntington, Long Island, to raid New London next morning. Temporarily ignoring the fact that he was also Sir Henry Clinton's secret courier, Gray joined the American troops, stripped to his shirt since the September day was hot, and fought through the first part of the battle. So fierce was the combat that Arnold was on the point of withdrawing his men when the Americans broke. Then Arnold was victorious. Gray barely escaped, and did not have time enough to get his coat, which probably contained his pass from Washington. He said later that, when he rode out of the fort gate, the British were twelve or fifteen rods behind him, and the ones in front fired at him "but overshot me." He would have been in real trouble if the redcoats had captured their own courier fighting against them, or if they had found the coat and the papers in it.

After two years as a double spy, Gray returned to the Continental Army. He may have been afraid he had given himself away in the fight at New London. Actually, the British seem never to have known what he was doing or how they had been deceived. Gray must have seemed to them just one more spy who had disappeared, as spies do. The Americans sent him off to Fort Wyoming (Wilkes Barre, Pennsylvania), where the British were not likely to get their hands on him.

Gray and Hunter were not the only American captains who were lending a "helping" hand to the British intelligence service, with General

Washington's full approval. Captain Caleb Bruen, of Newark, New Jersey, had been an eager patriot from the beginning of the Revolution, serving as Second Lieutenant in February, 1776, and rising to a captaincy by August. He had found it particularly annoying when, during an interval in this service, he was "shot at by the British while taking the cows to pasture."

After that year his name drops out of the war records for a long time. Then it reappears again. This time, however, the American Captain Bruen's name is in the British secret-service records. No one knows what he had been doing in the meantime. Probably he was busy convincing the British he was a complete traitor, like Benedict Arnold.

Captain Caleb Bruen, the New Jersey minuteman, now became Sir Henry Clinton's trusted courier and spy, operating all the way from his native New Jersey as far east as Rhode Island. His name does not appear in American army records again until 1783. Then he is arrested for illicit trading with the enemy—that is, blackmarketing. But one significant fact tells the story to the researcher reading the papers, which are now nearly two hundred years old. The man arrested with Bruen went before a court-martial at once. Bruen just disappears from the records. The next thing you know, the American government is paying him a pension for loyal service! So in the end, all New Jersey found out what the "traitor" had really been doing.

Though Sir Henry Clinton's exasperated intelligence officers knew well enough that there were leaks, they could not identify Captains Hunter, Gray, Bruen, or any of the other well-hidden American agents. They discovered the Culper line of communication across Long Island Sound (Caleb Brewster's whaleboats) almost as soon as it began to operate. A British officer prisoner, returning through Connecticut, had reported a number of whaleboats lying at Norwalk, "which pass over almost every night to Long Island." But this knowledge did the enemy no good, for there was no way for them to keep the boats from slipping across the Sound. Over a year passed before two British agents, working independently of each other, learned that Caleb Brewster commanded these whaleboats, which carried the spies' reports. Laying hands on Caleb was another matter. They never caught him.

Every intelligence agent working in a certain locality is almost bound to have an "opposite number"—that is, an enemy agent working against him. Brewster's opposite number in the British intelligence service was Nehemiah Marks, son of a prominent merchant in Derby, Connecticut. Marks went to New York almost as soon as the

Revolution began, to act as a "despatch agent" for
the British. From Long Island he made regular
secret crossings to Stamford and other Connecticut towns, partly to carry secret messages, partly
to spy. He avoided his native Derby, where he
would be recognized. People there knew nothing
about him except that he had "left town." Not
until the research for this book was undertaken
was it discovered *why* he had left town—a secret
kept from the 1770's to the 1950's! He left home
to work for the enemy. And of course as a Tory,
he never came back.

Nehemiah Marks reported several times that
Brewster was running dispatches for the Americans. Presently "Hiram the Spy" (William Heron,
of Redding, Connecticut) was also reporting on
Brewster. He wrote Clinton's headquarters:
"Private dispatches are frequently sent from
your city to the Chieftain here by some traitors.
They come by way of Setalket [Setauket], where
a certain Brewster receives them, at, or near a
certain woman's."

Learning at last how messages brought by
Brewster's whaleboats were carried through Connecticut, the British tried to figure out a way to
stop them. Nehemiah Marks offered to land with
British agents in Connecticut, lay an ambush
along the road, and capture the courier. But
this never happened. Perhaps the British com-

mand thought the plan was too risky. Perhaps Marks tried and failed. At any rate, nobody ever intercepted Brewster's dispatches.

A short time after this, in October, 1781, the British came still closer to the Culpers' secret. One of their spies, named Patrick Walker, took supper with Caleb Brewster in Fairfield, chatted a while, and even listened to Brewster tell of American plans for an attack on Floyd's Neck!

Walker had found the man who knew the facts. He had gotten him—perhaps a little drunk—to talking too much. He had learned a few of the patriots' secrets. But on the essential facts on which the safety of the whole Culper spy ring depended, Caleb Brewster—drunk or sober—was silent! Beyond a certain point, he would not speak.

The Culpers always knew their danger, but they never guessed how close the hangman's noose had dangled over their devoted heads the night those two "opposite" spies had supper together.

Not all double agents are loyal spies whose work for one side is just a pose to cover their real work for the other. Often a double agent is really a traitor to both sides, a contemptible rascal with no loyalty to anything, interested only in self and money.

William Heron of Redding, Connecticut, called

"Hiram the Spy," was a crafty fellow of this kind. The story of his treason—nearly as bad as Benedict Arnold's—remained a secret for a hundred years. Then, in 1882, a New York medical man, Dr. Thomas Emmett, brought to America two manuscript volumes, *Private Intelligence of Sir Henry Clinton*, which are now in the New York Public Library. These documents show that Heron was regularly supplying secret official information to the British, through Major Oliver DeLancey, who, after André's capture, was Sir Henry's intelligence officer. Heron was also providing Major General Samuel H. Parsons, of the American army, with supposedly secret British information, which General Parsons certainly thought "very valuable," as he reported to General Washington.

As a member of the Connecticut State Assembly, Heron knew all the secrets sent by the Continental Congress to the state officials. This information he passed on to Sir Henry Clinton. Sometimes he visited the British headquarters in New York openly. He seemed to be engaged in honest dealings on behalf of Connecticut, under a flag of truce. Actually, in addition to his legitimate business, he was betraying America's most secret affairs.

When Heron could not do this, he sent his secret reports by courier. In doing this he protected himself not by one "letter drop," but by two. (A letter drop is the place where one spy secretly leaves a message for another spy to pick up later. Neither man sees the other. Sometimes neither one has the least idea who the other is.)

Heron's method was to leave his message with one man (or woman). From this point a courier (who never saw Heron at all) took it to another man (or woman). At this point a British courier from New York City picked it up for Sir Henry. Thus the traitor Heron protected his own precious skin. The couriers would not betray him. They could not. They did not know who he was.

Much of Heron's information came through General Parsons. The general was a loyal American (though Heron was trying to corrupt him as Benedict Arnold had been corrupted). He was deceived into trusting Heron because the double-dealing rogue also spied on the British and passed his news on to the American general. When he was in New York under a flag of truce, he managed to get intelligence of the British forces. This he passed to General Parsons, who relayed it to General Washington. At least once Parsons praised the double spy highly for his valuable service to the American cause!

If either side had discovered what Heron was doing, either side would gladly have hanged him. But neither the British nor the Americans ever so much as suspected this shrewd and careful scoundrel. When the Americans won at last, the hypocrite was able to continue acting like a prominent and loyal Connecticut citizen. With no conscience to disturb him, he gave the impression of being a worthy and patriotic legislator. This illusory image remained undisturbed until Sir Henry Clinton's papers revealed him, long afterward, to have been a double spy—a traitor to both sides.

Main Action, and Spies on Each Side*

I. Spies in Massachusetts, 1775

Main Action: Battles of Lexington and Bunker Hill; British are besieged in Boston for nearly a year.

British Spies	American Spies
Benjamin Thompson, (Count Rumford)	Paul Revere's ring: Paul Revere; William Dawes; Joshua Bentley; Thomas Richardson; others.
Maj. Pitcairn	
Capt. Brown	
Ens. De Bernière	De Bonvouloir and d'Amboise, spies of France, later ally.
Lieut. Col. Smith	
John Howe	
Dr. Church	

II. Spies in New York, 1776

Main Action: Plots to kidnap Washington and start Tory uprising foiled; Battle of Long Island; British occupy New York City.

British Spies	American Spies
David Matthews, Tory mayor, N.Y.C.	Isaac Ketcham
William Tryon, Tory governor, N.Y.	William Corbie
	Nathan Hale
	Joshua Davis
Tory plotters' ring: Thomas Hickey; Priv. Lynch; James Mason; Gilbert Forbes; William Green; others.	Spy-catchers' ring: John Jay; Nathaniel Sackett; Col. Duer; Enoch Crosby; Dr. Miller; John Haines; Nicholas Brower.
Simon Mabie	
Dr. Prosser	
Enoch Hoag	
Silvester Handy	

---

* This list is of course incomplete; since many Tories and patriots in the colonies aided their own cause, a complete list of "spies" would run into hundreds.

III. Spies in New York, New Jersey and Pennsylvania, 1776-1777

Main Action: Washington retreats from New York; victories at
Trenton and Princeton; defeat at Brandywine; British occupy
Philadelphia; Burgoyne surrenders at Saratoga; British attack
at Whitemarsh fails.

British Spies
Samuel Wallis
Henry Williams
Francis Hogel
William Showers
Capt. Campbell
Daniel Taylor,
    silver-bullet courier

American Spies
Joshua and John Mersereau,
    family, and John Parker
John Honeyman
Lewis J. Costigin
Alexander Bryan
Intelligence officers:
    Lieut. Col. Reed; Maj. Gens.
    Stephen, Lincoln, Mifflin;
    Gens. Heath and Putnam;
    Cols. Boudinot and Dayton;
    Maj. Clark; Capts. Craig and
    McLane.
Mrs. Lydia Darragh, and son,
    button carrier

IV. Super Spies, 1778-1781

Main Action: General Howe resigns; British under General Clinton leave Philadelphia; French troops arrive at Newport;
Benedict Arnold burns New London.

British Spies
Intelligence officers:
    Capt. Beckit (Beckwith?);
    Col. Robinson; Maj. André;
    Maj. De Lancy
Nehemiah Marks
William Heron, "Hiram
    the Spy," double agent
Patrick Walker
Benedict Arnold

American Spies
Intelligence officers:
    Gen. Scott
    Maj. Tallmadge
"The Culpers":
    Robert Townsend,
    Samuel Woodhull
James Rivington
Caleb Brewster
Austin Roe
Capts. Hunter, Gray,
    Bruen, double agents